Poetry Crossing

50+ Lessons for 50 Years
of California Poets in the Schools

Phyllis Meshulam, Editor

Cathy Barber and Seretta Martin, Assistant Editors

Tresha Haefner and Richard Newsham, Field Editors

Copyright © 2014 by California Poets in the Schools
San Francisco, California
Printed in the United States of America
All rights reserved.

ISBN: 978-0-939927-55-5
Library of Congress PCN: 2014912878

First printing September 2014

Book design: Blake More
Cover artists: Mija Biggie, Meladie Cen, Cole Freeling, Alma Salyer, Willow Jakovac, Maya Sholin, Emma Van Horn, Stella Kenton-Braden, Francesca Mills, Aimee Gordon (all students from Mendocino County)

For Susan Herron Sibbet
1942–2013

*Our friend, fellow tiller of the classroom rows,
cheerleader, visionary*

Contents

Foreword 6
Introduction 7

Mostly for Younger

Wannabes (Metaphor) 10
The Moon's the North Wind's Cooky: A Warm-Up on Metaphor & Simile 12
Warm-Up Exercises for the Five Senses and Details 13
Color Our World with Poems 14
Hands and Hearts (Chant) 16
Rain Poems in Several Voices 18
Magic Bag (Simile, Imagination) 20
Breathe In, Breathe Out 22
Moon Poems 24
In the Center of the Drum (Chant and Rhythm) 26
The No-Plan Plan 28
Poems on Poems (*Ars Poetica*: The Art of Poetry) 30

Mostly in the Middle

Secret Place 34
The Shy Sky (Personification) 36
Grand Slam Poetry (Hyperbole) 38
Apples to Apples (Juxtaposition) 40
Sensing the Way Home: Using Maps to Remember Every Detail 42
Making a Poem Hum: Combining Alliteration with Onomatopoeia 44
On the Other Side of . . . (Repetition and Concrete Details) 46
The Fish 48
Entering a Picture: Poetry from Visual Art 50
Word Pictures and Hieroglyphics: The Birth of Writing 52
Japanese Tanka: From the Concrete to the Ephemeral 54
The Poem Is in Your Life (Memory) 56
Wild Mind (Chant: Slant and Internal Rhyme) 58
Where Poems Hide (Personification, Anaphora, Narrative) 60
My Heart 62
Pantoums (Repetition) 64
Mind of Tumbling Water (Line Breaks) 66
Writing Like Sappho (Sapphic Modernism) 68
Who's Your Muse? 70
Music Magic (Onomatopoeia, Lyricism) 72
The Heart's Book of Records (Superlatives) 74
I Am (Metaphor, Chant) 76
Let Us Gather in a Flourishing Way (Bilingual Rhythms) 78
Glorious Color Odes 80
Insecure About Sestinas? (Sestina, Enjambment) 82
Ode to a Quality (Ode, Adjectives, Synesthesia) 84
If That Picture Could Speak . . . (Ekphrasis) 86

Inspired by the Chinese (Shi) 88
Riddles for All Ages 90
Poetry in the Science Class (Rhyme, Couplets, Metaphor) 92

Mostly for Older

Playing with Sound Strategies (Assonance, Consonance, and Rhyme) 96
Poems for Paintings (Ekphrasis) 98
We Believe in Poetry 100
Imagery, Fantasy, and Freedom (Imagery, Narrative) 102
Crisis in the Classroom (Juxtaposition) 104
Opening the Heart on Paper (Metaphor/Simile) 106
The Anti-Ode 108
Emotions: First-Time Experience, Loss of Innocence 110
Detailed Memories: Emotions Triggered by an Object or Event 112
The Power of Negative Space 114

Acknowledgments 116
Credits 117
Illustrations 122
Recommended Resources for Teachers 123
CPitS Mission 124

Foreword

The Heart's Book of Records

"I love the dim moon. I love the immense kindness." Victoria, a six-year-old girl with a faraway look in her eyes, wrote these words at an after-school poetry workshop at her public library. I think this immense kindness lives at the heart of California Poets in the Schools.

We do our best to create a home for children of every age, to help them feel safe to discover and to allow their souls and hearts to venture forth in words in a realm where there is no judgment and no grades, only encouragement and enthusiasm. You will sense this in *Poetry Crossing*, a far-reaching offering of poet-teacher lesson plans, and sample poems by student poets, poet-teachers, and some great poets from around the world. And you will learn some of our secrets here.

CPitS has become a gathering place for many of us who've been scribbling poems on the margins of the world since we were children and who now find ourselves helping children scribble their own, sometimes life-saving, poems. We have all come together around our love of language, and we bring this love to children right where they live. Here's a glimpse of Alex Intara's poem about baseball: "It's stars bursting on top of second base. / Baseball of thunder roaring. / Baseball of foggy nights. . . . / It's a blue meteor falling." We are taken out into nature in the group poem "Creek Sestina": "The water over rocks makes them play leapfrog; / the water echoes like a kid splashing in a canyon." Though as writers we may sometimes scribble on the margins, our work in CPitS is not marginal but central to the human heart and to the core purpose of teaching literacy: helping others find a way to experience profound communication and connection through writing and reading.

For many of us, California Poets in the Schools has become home in the truest sense of the word. In the realm of poems, we deeply hear one another's heart, mind, and soul. Listen to the renowned Yiddish poet Rachel Korn, whose words take us back to a long-ago place of childhood: "On the other side of the poem my mother may appear / and stand in the doorway awhile lost in thought, / then call me home as she used to call me home long ago, . . ." And here's student Vincent "Burtsie" Maruffo, writing in "My Road Back Home": "I will make it / back home / for the moon / won't leave me / alone."

Such poems don't usually appear out of nowhere. And here's where we share our secrets: in these fifty plus inspiring and clearly laid-out lesson plans, including "Mind of Tumbling Water," "Glorious Color Odes," and "The Heart's Book of Records." Each lesson provides a framework or structure that allows students' creativity to find form. I like to call the outcome "controlled abandon": inner discoveries shaped in a poem that can be read by others. In this sense, all of our poems—adults' and students'—can be our "heart's book of records." Our poems allow us to experience the joy of hearing and being heard. We find our needs and longings are all the same, and we develop new love and respect both for ourselves and for each other.

Welcome, enjoy, dive in, and partake of this book, which celebrates fifty years of the collected wisdom of California Poets in the Schools. Live with us in the immense kindness, where children lead the way.

> **—Susan G. Wooldridge, author of *poemcrazy: freeing your life with words*
> (Random House, 1996), now in its twenty-sixth printing**

Editor's Note:

Not only does poem-making open our hearts and record what lies inside, but it is an inspiring way to learn "Common Core" skills. For example: alliteration, similes, rhymes, metaphors and repeated lines; how to use figurative language such as personification; make transitions; use concrete words and phrases, descriptive and sensory details; use precise language concisely; write narratives, write on a regular basis, revise . . .

Introduction

Readers, it's good to meet you at the *Poetry Crossing!* This crossroads represents evolutions (California Poets in the Schools' over fifty years), epiphanies (the authors' as poet-teachers), and the journey in every included poem.

As a young substitute teacher weighing what to do with my life, I often pulled my copy of Kenneth Koch's *Wishes, Lies, and Dreams: Teaching Children to Write Poetry* from my backpack to use in class. Based on Koch's experiences as a visiting poet, the book was full of sample poems from New York City elementary schoolchildren. I was in Los Angeles high schools where the hunger for poetry was also very much alive. The age chasm didn't matter. Only slightly reengineered, the seeds of Koch's lessons bore fruit in those classrooms.

Bear this in mind as you find your way through our book. The section "Mostly for Younger" has some lessons with variations for up to twelfth grade. So does the sprawling section "Mostly in the Middle," though it's primarily for third through eighth graders. And there are a few lesson plans that honestly promise "for all ages."

We at CPitS blush with the following honor: the generosity of so many living poets who have given us the right to reprint their work. This supportive team includes Pulitzer Prize winner Gary Snyder; two former U.S. poets laureate, Robert Hass and Ted Kooser; our current California poet laureate, Juan Felipe Herrera, and a previous one, Al Young. It also includes Jane Hirshfield (a finalist for the National Book Critics Circle Award); Brenda Hillman (a winner of the Griffin Poetry Prize); Genny Lim, winner of the American Book Award; Mexican poet Alberto Blanco, a recipient of a Guggenheim grant; Ellen Bass, winner of a Pushcart Prize; David St. John, a winner of a Prix de Rome fellowship; and Bruce Weigl, a winner of the Robert Creeley Award.

Our format—each lesson distilled into a page of procedures coupled with one worksheet—doesn't leave much room for the why and how of getting started. The remainder of this introduction features words of wisdom on that theme from several poet-teachers. —**Phyllis Meshulam**

Why should we teach poetry? Confidence in writing: Teachers often tell me that a previously reluctant writer found poetry to be the necessary catalyst for engaging in other kinds of writing. *Freedom:* While a poem may be a far cry from a structured essay, it can be the first step in getting a student *interested* in writing. *Discovery of self:* In crafting poems, young writers find what they need to say about themselves. They get to choose the exact words that fit and express their sometimes quirky personalities. *Economy and grace with language:* The best possible result of practicing writing is beautiful writing. *Catharsis and celebration:* Whatever we have within us will be transformed as it becomes a poem. —**Dan Levinson**

Introducing poetry. While I must have a time structure to my lessons, I need to promote a sense of timelessness, of being in a moment of ferment, of total possibility. Within the students' imaginations, anything could happen. For many years I used the ploy of speechlessly beginning the session by walking to the board and beginning to write out the model poem on the board, as though unfurling a flag. In a sense, this is performance. I give a dramatic reading of the poems I bring in. Poetry, when presented evocatively, is mesmerizing. It's the heart of language. If it's a well-chosen poem, it will emanate the creative spirit. The students will want to get back there with their own words. —**Grace Grafton**

On discussions: appreciating, not analyzing. Do yourselves and the kids a favor. Don't require them to participate in a discussion analyzing great poems. You can point out age-appropriate deliciousness. But mainly allow students to respond to this question: "What were some of your favorite parts in this poem?" —**Phyllis Meshulam**

On making the transition from listening to the poem to actually writing. I give starters, because the most challenging transition of a poetry session is when kids have to begin their poems. Helping them to maintain focus is vital to teaching a successful lesson. This is true for anyone. That first line, that initial phrase—if the writer can "hear" or "get" that, the rest usually follows fairly easily. If kids say, "I don't know what I want to write," I talk with them, ask them if there was anything they liked about the example poem or anything they remember about the group discussion, until they say something interesting, then that's their beginning. Sometimes I write down their words as they speak. —**Grace Grafton**

Sharing aloud. No matter that you have seen poems materialize on kids' papers that you would like to shout from the rooftops. There will be young people who stand at the front of the room, open their mouths, and are then completely inaudible. Here is my favorite intervention. As I introduce the read-aloud portion of the lesson, I say, "You do know that our voices make waves? We can't see them, but scientists can measure them. Think of your voice as a swimmer who needs a good strong push to swim from one side of the pool to the other. When it gets there, it must get out of the pool and jump up and down on the far eardrums of the room as if they were a trampoline!" Talking about the physics of sound makes this a less emotionally fraught process and helps many students. As the read-aloud time goes on, someone will revert back, or the heater will come on. Then just say, "Uh-oh, your voice will have to make bigger waves than that to be heard. It is in danger of drowning before it gets beyond those first desks. Give it an extra push." —**Phyllis Meshulam**

Limits of freedom. What if your students want to journey to dark places in their poems or explore subjects that aren't normally talked about? Poetry needs to be a safe place where young writers can experiment with their thoughts and feelings in order to grow. But the same boundaries that exist everywhere else in school can be designated in the realm of writing; it's your job to remind students of these boundaries. When a student reads a new poem out loud whose subject matter crosses some invisible line, I good-naturedly point out that there's a time and place for everything, and ask the classroom teacher to back me up. —**Dan Levinson**

Giving feedback. One important thing that I learned is that if students are made to feel good about their writing, they'll want to write. So feedback is important and is also tricky. With kids, I always focus on what's working. I actually do that with adults, too. Everyone's ego can be fragile. Students have trouble separating their poems from themselves, and whether they act tough or not, they can get hurt by criticism. And yet critiquing is a vital part of the process. It's also a form of validation. It's not enough to just put a sticker on the poem; students need to hear that someone in the class, besides the teacher and me, liked something about their poem and could relate to it. I have kindergarteners giving feedback to their classmates. It actually helps them to listen if they know they will be asked to say what they liked or repeat what they heard. —**Shelley Savren**

Revision. A poem is a story on a diet: every word matters. To prepare students for revision, which literally means to see again, I say that a poem is like a diamond in the rough: it needs careful polishing to bring out all its facets. A poem is like the body: toss out those junk food words; look for the spine from which to hang your poem, then give it some muscle. I use a teaching structure that is both directed and organic. I tell students the rules are meant to be changed; they owe allegiance to the integrity of the poem, not the assignment of the day. —**Maureen Hurley**

Silence. I used to think my most important job was to get students to write until an eighth-grade teacher said, "Sometimes the right to silence is as powerful as the right to write" and broke the spell. So when the fearless and inventive sixth grader became a silent seventh grader, I could be patient until he morphed into an eighth-grade creative writer. But usually we CPitS teachers don't get to work with the same students for multiple years. So I often start class with sixty seconds of no writing (thirty seconds of quiet mind and thirty seconds observing whatever enters), and then I can't stop them from writing. Some students can't even wait that long. That makes me happy; the sound of their pencils scratching and zooming across paper makes me happy. Writers at work: the best music there is. —**Gwynn O'Gara**

Listen: you will hear echoes of that music as you read this book. And soon, you will hear it again in your own classrooms.

Mostly for Younger

Wannabes (Metaphor)
For Kindergarten Through Grade Eight

by Julie Hochfeld

Magic. Poetry is magic. Where else can chalk become a caterpillar, a stapler an alligator, and an eraser a chunk of gold? On the first day of class, I introduce similes and metaphors, hold up classroom objects, and have students compare them to other things. Then I tell the class that, with imagination, their pencils will become magic wands. "Wannabes," which is a great first lesson but can also be taught later, takes the art of comparison in a new direction. Students stretch their imaginations as they speak for animate or inanimate objects, transform them into other things, and show how they want to be different, and sometimes grander, than they are.

1. Introduce similes and metaphors, as suggested above.
2. Ask students what they think a Wannabe is. Then share definitions from the dictionary. With young students, give a simple definition.
3. Read the sample poems aloud. Students can take turns reading, or if they are young, the teacher and/or poet-teacher can read.
4. Play the Wannabe game. Hold up classroom objects and have students describe what these might want to be. You can help elaborate on the fantasies. Anything can be a Wannabe!
5. From here, you can: (a) write a group Wannabe poem; (b) write a group poem and then write individual poems, this session or the next; or (c) move directly to individual writing.
6. If you begin with a group poem, have the class brainstorm five ideas, then vote on one. Group poems are great for emergent writers and/or students with lesser skills. But if you have limited time and capable writers, go directly to individual writing. You can still write brainstormed ideas on the board to get ideas flowing. And then write, write, write!
7. If you are using a collection of objects (see below), the students can choose their objects now. I don't usually bring in special objects, but they could inspire some students.
8. Prompts, which can be written and/or spoken (an abbreviated version is on the worksheet):
   - Pick a subject, either something in the classroom or in your imagination, and write about what else that subject wants to be.
   - Look at or think about your subject. What does it remind you of?
   - Use the five senses. What else could your subject look, sound, taste, smell, or feel like? Be specific. What does it want to be or do, wish it were, dream of being, pretend to be, long to be, imagine, and/or secretly desire? For instance, a shoe might want to be a boat or a race car.
   - Write many short comparisons or one long comparison. Use clear details.
   - Your poem can end happily, acknowledging your subject is good as it is, end with a sad reality, or end with your subject still wanting more . . .
   - Write as if you are the subject, or write about it (first person or third person).
9. When the writing period is over, share the poems. If there is time, classmates can give at least one specific, positive comment for each poem.
10. I believe in the power of samples. Each time you teach this lesson, you can save strong samples. Teach poems you like that approach the same theme in a variety of ways.

(Thank you to Jacqueline Sweeney, whose book *Teaching Poetry: Yes You Can!*, and Lillian Morrison, whose poem "Surf" first inspired me to write this lesson.)

Time and Materials: The lesson will take forty-five to sixty minutes, or longer for two rounds of writing. Bring a collection of interesting objects, use classroom objects, and/or rely on students' imaginations.

Worksheet

A Wish
by Estelle Fuller, Humboldt County

A lizard wants to be a dragon.
It wants to have wings
that slice through the air
like a knife.

When it opens its mouth,
it wants to feel hot flames
rushing up to dissipate
in the cold air.

It wants to be giant,
to burst from its glass tank
and leave the pet shop
for a cave in the mountains.

It wants the fine sand
in its tank
to be large piles of gold
that knights try to reclaim
only to be burnt to a crisp.

But all it can do
is bask in the artificial heat
of the lamp.
And wait for its turn to fly.

Fireworks That Wished They Were
by Cathryn Noel-Veatch, Humboldt County

Fireworks want to be everlasting,
like stars in the night.
They want to be rainbows,
low enough for a child to touch.

Fireworks wish they could
be a multicolored bird
that could be seen all the time.

Fireworks wish they could
be used more often,
other than the Fourth of July.

But fireworks are lucky:
they are enjoyed
for the time they are
up in the dark midnight sky.

Wanna Be Bigger
by Kieran McNulty, Humboldt County

My chihuahua wants to be a lion
with its loud roar,
or a huge, strong bear.

My chihuahua wants to be called a predator.
My chihuahua wants big teeth and claws.
My chihuahua wants to be bigger.

Chihuahuas want to rule the world.
Chihuahuas want to be tigers stalking deer.

But instead, they are usually called
"Fifi" or "Wiwi."

Their barks sound like
high-pitched fire alarms.
And they are smaller than footballs.

Advice to Writers
Choose an interesting subject.
Then let your imagination soar!

- Use the five senses.
  What else could your subject
  look, smell, taste, feel, or sound like?
- What might your subject want to be
  or do, wish it were, dream of being,
  pretend to be, long to be, imagine, or secretly desire?
- You can write many short comparisons or one long one.
- Your poem can end with acceptance, a sad reality,
  or with your subject still wanting more.
- Be specific. Poetry comes alive in details.
- Most important, be creative and have fun!

The Moon's the North Wind's Cooky: A Warm-Up on Metaphor & Simile, For Kindergarten Through Grade Four

by Seretta Martin (inspired by Karen Benke)

On the first or second day of a poetry workshop, I like to do this fun warm-up with younger poets so they can start to understand what goes into a poem and what makes it different from a story (prose).

Post a large chart with the definitions of both *metaphor* and *simile*. Tell the students, "We will be writing a poem, but first, we are going to practice using something very important in poetry: metaphors and similes. They both compare things, but in different ways." Pointing to the chart, say, "Writers use metaphors to surprise the reader of their poem. They are magical and help the reader to see two things at once."

1. Read the two definitions and point out how similes use *like* or *as*, while metaphors say one thing is another thing. Call on a "firefly" to turn down the lights as you project the following list of lines on a screen and say, "Now it's time to play a game. Read and listen to these lines carefully so you can tell me if each line has a simile or a metaphor. What two things are being compared? Raise your hand when you know the answer."
   - My sister's tongue is a long country road, wet and bumpy.
   - I wandered lonely as a cloud.
   - The baby was like an octopus, grabbing at all the toys on the shelves.
   - The giant's steps were thunder as he ran toward Jack. (Be careful, this one is tricky.)
   - The bar of soap was a slippery eel during the dog's bath.
   - Ted was as nervous as a cat with a long tail in a room full of rocking chairs.
   - The man's teeth are like a white fence that holds in a pink dog.
   - My soul was once a fierce polar bear, and now it is a gentle child.
   - My puppy is a kiss in the rain.
   - Her hair is like a jungle of twisted vines.
   - My baby sister's fingers are like worms poking me in the eye.
   - As the teacher entered the room, she muttered under her breath, "This class is like a three-ring circus!"
2. Now, ask the students to come up with lines of their own and raise their hands to say them out loud
3. Read the following poems together, identifying the similes and metaphors. Comment on the images. Point to stanzas and tell them that a stanza is to poetry what a paragraph is to prose, but poems use more concise language. Ask if there are any questions.

Materials: Definition chart for metaphors and similes, projector and screen or white board.

The Moon's the North Wind's Cooky
by Vachel Lindsay

The Moon's the North Wind's cooky.
He bites it, day by day,
Until there's but a rim of scraps
That crumble all away.

The South Wind is a baker.
He kneads clouds in his den,
And bakes a crisp new moon *that . . . greedy*
North . . . Wind . . . eats . . . again!

Fog
by Carl Sandburg

The fog comes
on little cat feet.

It sits looking
over harbor and city
on silent haunches
and then moves on.

Warm-Up Exercises for the Five Senses and Details For Grades One Through Five

by Cathy Barber

This is a good way for young students to be reminded of the five senses and of how important they are to good writing. I usually use this exercise on my first day with a group.

1. Ask the students whether they know the five ways that we perceive the world. How do we know what is going on around us? Our body has five ways to learn about the world—what are they? As the students correctly identify the senses and then name them, write them on the board: taste, touch, sight, sound, smell.
2. Ask the students to close their eyes, and create a little vignette for them. (I admit my scene is more than a little *Ozzie and Harriet*, so if you want to update or change it, by all means do so. Replace the mother with a father, replace the chocolate chip cookies with another food, the dog with a cat or a hamster, or make it a drive to the donut shop. Change it however you like, as long as you get all five senses in the scene.) Tell the students to imagine they are coming home from school:

   "You arrive at the sidewalk in front of your house. You can hear the *tick tick* of your shoes on the walk. You climb the steps to the front door, and you hear your dog barking excitedly inside. Once the door is open, your dog jumps on you, and you feel the scratch of its claws on your skin, not enough to break the skin, just a scratch. You smell chocolate, and you walk to the kitchen, where your mother greets you with, 'Hello, welcome home.' You see an orange plate with three cookies on the wooden table, a glass of milk beside the plate. You pull out a chair to sit down, and it makes a screech across the floor. You pick up the glass of milk and feel the beads of condensation on the glass, the coolness of the milk, and you take a bite of the first cookie and it tastes sooooo good, like chocolate and butter, and sweet. You take a drink of the cool milk to wash it down."

3. Now tell them to open their eyes and name the sensory details from the scene and which sense each illustrates. They are usually incredibly good at this and remember almost every sensory detail from the vignette.
4. Tell them that the more they use sensory details in their poems, the more the reader will understand and feel their poem. I often then segue into a little exercise on details.
5. Ask: "If I told you I saw a car on the way to your school, what kind of car was it?" They start to give me their ideas, usually a red sports car. Ask: "What if I told you it was a very old yellow car . . . (*pause*) with a dented-in fender . . . (*pause*) and a bad exhaust that blew smoke out the back? (*Pause.*) And it made a noise like *chug, chug, chug,* and the driver was honking the horn?"
6. Tell the students that if they include a car in their poem, they should add details so the reader will see the red sports car they intend and not the "chug, chug, chug" car you just described. And the same is true for every other object in their poems. A cat? Is it a fat black cat? An orange kitten? A tabby? The moon? Is it a full moon or a little sliver?

I usually teach place poems after these warm-ups, but you could teach anything that uses the senses and details.

Color Our World with Poems
For Kindergarten Through Grade Three

by Karen K. Lewis

(This lesson has been adapted from ideas shared by poet-teacher Karin Faulkner, with a nod to Kenneth Koch's pioneering work in New York City during the 1960s.)

We connect with colors at an early age. In this lesson, the classroom comes alive with colors and colorful language. What sound does purple make? What does red taste like? We'll play with images, similes, synesthesia, sounds, and alliteration to create a colorful kaleidoscope of creative poems. This project engages younger students and can be adapted for higher grades. Students may turn their poems into visual art: drawings, color mobiles, or a classroom collage.

1. Set up a blank wall board, or tape a blank scroll of paper on the board.
2. Have students sit in a semicircle so they can all see the board and each other.
3. Chat about how poets connect colors to objects, actions, sounds, and feelings. Read the stanza of Federico García Lorca's "Sleepwalking Ballad" on the worksheet. Prompt the students to brainstorm how to connect a color word with something else: *Brown ___. Brown is like ___. Blue sounds like___. Green jumps like a frog. Purple ___, purple ___.*
4. Ask children to raise their hands and share an idea. Write each image on the board/scroll. Once you have five to ten ideas, read the lines together and ask students to dream up extra details to add. Example: *Brown is like a bear that ___.* (Ask: What is your bear doing?) Mention that the best poems mix real things with "make believe."
5. Applaud students for sharing creative details.
6. Ask students to create a title; this might be two words connected in a fun new way.
7. Tell students: "Now we will each have a chance to write our own color poem."
8. Dismiss students to their desks and hand out paper and pencils.
9. Remind students that this is silent writing time. Tell them: "Write your own poem about color. Ask your imagination for images and feelings that go with your color."
10. Circulate around the classroom. Remind young poets to work in silence, or to raise their hand if they want help. Encourage "stuck" students by asking them their favorite color. Suggest: "[Favorite color] is like [feeling, sound, object, or creature]." Let students know they can fix spelling later. Optional: Pass out paint sample color strips as students are writing. Mention they might find new ideas from these colors or (grades two and up) from the color names on the paint strips.
11. About two minutes before silent writing ends, ask students to dream up titles. Encourage vivid language: "Titles don't need to make sense. Sometimes poets make a surprise or use a secret for their title."
12. Return to the circle. Take turns sharing poems aloud. Practice being a good audience, with careful listening and polite applause.
13. Express thanks to your young writers for creating a colorful new world.

Time and Materials: Allow 45 to 60 minutes. You will need a scroll and markers for the warm-up group poem, pencils, and writing paper. Optional: color strips from a paint store, and/or art supplies, plus parent helpers for students who need extra help.

Worksheet

Romance Sonámbulo
(extracto, estrofa dos)
by Federico García Lorca

   Verde que te quiero verde.
Grandes estrellas de escarcha,
vienen con el pez de sombra
que abre el camino del alba.
La higuera frota su viento
con la lija de sus ramas,
y el monte, gato garduño,
eriza sus pitas agrias.
Pero ¿quién vendra? ¿Y por dónde?...
Ella sigue en su baranda,
Verde carne, pelo verde,
soñando en la mar amarga.

Sleepwalker's Ballad
(excerpt, stanza two)

   Green, how I love you green.
Great glittering stars of frost
come with the fish of shadows
that open the road to dawn.
The fig tree rubs the wind
with the sandpaper of its branches,
and the mountain, thieving cat,
bristles its sour agaves.
But who will arrive? And from where?...
She follows along her balcony railing,
green skin, green hair,
dreaming in the bitter sea.

(Translated by Karen Lewis)

Silver
  by Greyson Gove, Marin County

Silver is small and shy
He is invisible to those who don't believe
Silver flies on wings of woven stars
He watches from a peak of silver snow
He uses his magic for good only
He wears a cloak of moonbeams
      and a tunic of mist
When he's sad he takes a ride on a shooting star
      to cheer him up
When he's happy he glows and shines
He dreams of becoming a star.

Dream Colors
  by Nayeli Orozco, Mendocino County

Purple looks like a book.
Blue feels like blueberries.
Pink tastes like a pink cookie.
Red sounds like my heart.
Green is like green grass.
Black is like the dots on a ladybug.
Green is like a leaf.
Purple is my color of my dreams.

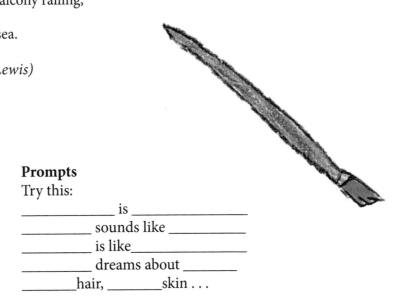

Prompts
Try this:
_____ is _____
_____ sounds like _____
_____ is like_____
_____ dreams about _____
_____hair, _____skin . . .

California Poets In The Schools

Hands and Hearts (Chant)
For All Ages
by Karen K. Lewis

(This lesson was inspired by Susan Sibbet's very kinetic approach with kindergartners, and by Karin Faulkner's and Maureen Hurley's work with older students.)

One element that sets humans apart from other animals is our ability to use our hands to create and to communicate. While today most poems are written down, ancient peoples often created their poems out loud when they sat around the fire and spoke chants. The repetitive form of a chant encourages emergent readers and writers. More experienced writers can take this project in many directions, including the negative poem, which would assert, *My hands cannot . . .* You might begin in a warm-up circle playing hand and clapping games. Students take turns to call out a word while they clap once. Older students could start by drawing an outline of their hands, then filling in the design with symbols, words, and colors to express the powers of their hands.

1. Start by sitting in a circle. Share Nancy Wood's hands chant from the worksheet aloud.
2. Ask students to think about things they can do with their hands. Then ask what they *wish* they could do. Go around the circle and take turns speaking a word. As each idea is spoken, ask the entire class to clap once. This establishes a nice group spirit. (In alternative schools or juvenile detention, this can be a powerful, healing, expressive process if the writers have gotten into trouble with their hands.) Note: If you have students with physical limitations, you might adapt the project to a different part of the body. My feet, my thumb, etc.
3. For young students, create a class chant on the board in the style of the hands chant. Encourage students to add a mixture of real and pretend ideas: "My hands will . . ." "My hands remember . . ." "My hands wish . . ." After composing a group poem, brainstorm a title.
4. Older students may skip the circle and start by looking at the sample poems on the worksheet and at Jane Hirshfield's "A Hand."
5. At their seats, students can draw their hands in outline.
6. Next is silent creative time. Encourage students to write their own poems about hands. Instruct young writers to try the chant form; also suggest that they alter their pattern at the end to create a surprise. More fluent writers might imagine wild connections; allow them to be inventive in whatever ways they choose.
7. When students finish writing—if they have not already drawn their hand outlines—ask them to do so. Prompt them to fill their hands with symbols from their poems and from their lives. The symbols may include real things as well as dreams. Inspire inventive colors and patterns, jewelry, scars, special powers, tattoos, souvenirs of journeys, talents, cultural heritage. Be clear about your boundaries for using art materials: ink on the paper, not on skin!
8. Dream up great titles; go beyond "My Hands" to something more unique.
9. Sharing time might include spoken poems and/or clapping games, as well as an art exhibition or installation.

Materials: Binder paper, pencils for writing poems, plain white paper for tracing hands, a variety of colored pens and drawing pens to add designs to hands art. Optional: a white board (or scroll) to create a K through second-grade group poem; collage materials to embellish the finished hands poems for reluctant artists; Jane Hirshfield's "A Hand," from *Given Sugar, Given Salt*, Harper Collins. For inspiring sounds during writing time, try R. Carlos Nakai's Native American flute music.

Worksheet

[Untitled]
by Nancy C. Wood

With these hands
I have held a bird with a broken wing.
With these hands
I have touched my children in the sun.
With these hands I have made
a house of living earth.
With these hands
I have worked a field of growing corn.
With these hands I have learned to kill
As much as I have learned to live.
These hands are the tools of my spirit.
These hands are the warriors of my anger.
These hands are the limitations of my self.
These hands grow old and feel
unfamiliar walls
As they reach out to find
the world I used to know.

My Hands Are Everything
by Lauren Raith, Marin County

My hand is a rocking sea
My hand is a black-winged dove
My hand crawls like a black spider
My hand closes like a turtle
My hands remember my hamster
My hands are sewing the big blue blanket
   above you
My hands hold the Earth so it does not fall
My hands will reach to the fluffy white
   clouds

Mi Mano
  by Aldo Encizo, San Francisco County

*Mi mano es
El corazón de
Mis padres palpitando
Y era de mi
Abuelita querida*

*Mi mano es como
Las caricias que
Mis padres me
Dan siempre
Antes de
Dormir*

*Mi mano es
La sangre que corre
En mis venas
Siempre y también
En el corazón*

*Mi mano es
Como una cascada
Brillante y
Osos comiendo
Pececillos de
Oro brillante.*

My Hand

My hand is
The heart of
My parents beating
And it was that of
My dear grandmother

My hand is like
The caresses that
My parents always
Give me before
I go to
Sleep

My hand is
The blood that runs
In my veins
Always and also
In my heart

My hand is
Like a brilliant
Waterfall and
Bears eating
Little shining
Golden fish.

*(Translated by
Jim Cartwright, poet-teacher)*

Prompts
Try these starters: My hands can . . . My hands wish . . . With these hands . . . If I lost my hands . . . My hands remember . . . My hands will . . . These hands are . . .

California Poets In The Schools

Rain Poems in Several Voices For Elementary Grades

by Alice Pero

This lesson works because it does not require even basic English skills. A child who does not speak English well can write phonetic sounds for the Voice 2 part and come away feeling she accomplished something in the class. Almost every child knows the language of the rain!

1. Start with a drum, making rhythms. Each child gets a turn.
2. Have the children read the Sibbet poem, taking turns with the various parts. (Since this poem doesn't fit on the worksheet, you may wish to project it or copy it onto chart paper.)
3. In a large class, this reading is done in groups, but give one child the Voice 3 part. The others make rain sounds. In Sibbet's poem, the Voice 3 is the main part and the other voices are the sounds. Read the Voice 3 part first, then add the other Voices for interesting sound effects.*
4. Brainstorm some rain sounds. As students think of sounds, write them on the board, showing how the sounds might be spelled. Get more spellings from the students. Let them play with this; it isn't rote!
5. Now, have the children write poems about rain. They will alternate between writing the "Rain Poem" part and the "Rain Sounds" part.
6. Perform the poems. Practice getting to the point where Voice 1 is heard distinctly and the other parts are interesting sound effects. Voice 1 can read alone first, then Voice 2 joins in on a second read through. If time allows, practice having Voice 1 read a line alone, then Voice 2 join in on the next line, then silent again, then join in again etc. If time allows, add sounds with small percussion instruments. Experiment with sounds!

Materials: A drum, other small percussion instruments. The Sibbet poem, in a form that it can be shared.

*Sibbet performed this starting with Voice 1, followed by Voice 2. Then the more narrative Voice 3 came in, repeating her/his lines in reverse order one time.

Rain Suite

by Susan Sibbet, poet-teacher
(to be read aloud as a trio of voices)

Voice 1

Sip, Sip, Slip, lip,
sip, sip,
Sssh, shhh, shhh, wish, this
Wish, wish, shh
[Keep repeating until Voice 3 is done.]

Voice 2

blink blank, not
sock, clock, knock
not knock, not,
dark, lock, like, not
light, dot, dot,
blink, plank, not
[Keep repeating until Voice 3 is done.]

Voice 3 *[Speak very clearly.]*

Hollow   sound
                     of metal
                        dripping
drainpipe
                  water
rattling with the rain
            sound   echoing

in the light well
in the narrow
                  space
between two buildings

         this rain
in the dark
            early morning
winter rain
before we open our eyes

Worksheet

Rain Poem – Voice 1
by Audrey Kim, L.A. County

Slip! I fall down
I can't use machine
I don't like rain
I hate rain
But the sound is beautiful—
Slup blup Tub
Can you hear it?
Like the small mouse is talking
Wow—look at the window—
There are ummm . . .
Yellow Green Red Blue
Colorful umbrellas!!
Now I will like the rain

Rain Sounds – Voice 2

blink plunk blank
see sss ss
fank sank bank
ssss—sss—ss—
boulk poolk dink
Heeeee   seeee beeee
Al Dl El
Rak Dak Palk
Bleeee———
Flup Sew Doe
Plup———

Water Running . . . Voice 1
by Imogen Dayton, L.A. County

Water running through the mountains,
splashing up and down
Rolling in the hills with snowflakes all around
Streaming through the meadow
with snowflakes falling down
Bells far off, strong
with rings of rain far off
in the wintery rain

Rain Sounds – Voice 2

Drip pop drip splash drip drop drig
Splash pop pop splash
Drip dir pop drip splash

Rain – Voice 1
by Lance Doven, L.A. County

Rain is falling, washing my ears
I try to listen to the thunder but I cannot hear
For the rain is around me, making its sound
Yet it hits so lightly on the soft, soft ground
The rain never stopping, it seems like forever
when will it stop?
Maybe never

Rain Sounds – Voice 2

Swish, Swish
Blup, pup choo
You chip gee flip
Nee trip zoo
Flop flop sheoeshoe shoe shoe sheoe shoes show
Kerpank! Kerplunk! Ply tup!

Rain Is Falling . . . Voice 1
by Charlie Gerson, L.A. County

The rain is falling
The smoke is scattering
into ashes
burning out the flames
before the water hits the ground
and it burns the flames out
The rain is roaring on the mountainside

Rain Sounds – Voice 2

Swish drip swish
Drip Splat swish drip swish
Splash drip Splat

Advice to Writers

Rain makes lots of different noises.
Try to remember the way rain sounds.
This will help you
with your rain poem and rain sounds

Magic Bag (Simile, Imagination) For Preschool Through Grade Two

by Arthur Dawson

(This lesson was inspired by Irwin Rosen, Susan Terence, and Melissa Kwasny.)

This lesson uses children's love of mystery and surprise by revealing and exploring the items in a Magic Bag to create a group poem. (My Magic Bag is from India and has colorful designs and round mirrors.) Items can include both everyday and unusual things, like a rain stick, a Tibetan singing bowl, a wooden spoon, a can opener, a turtle-shaped ocarina flute, an egg slicer, and so on. It's good if each item can do something that makes it come alive, like make a sound or dance in the air. I like to use this activity as part of a first lesson. It works best with the students sitting knee-to-knee on a rug.

1. Beforehand: Choose a scribe, either teacher or aide, and give him or her a pad of paper, a pencil, and the instruction to just catch the gist of students' ideas—no need for complete sentences. The scribe doesn't need to start writing until No. 2 and/or No. 7, below. For now, keep your Magic Bag hidden from the students.
2. During this first session, we often warm up by making up alphabet poems: looking at letters and making up visual metaphors for what they could be. Large cutouts on stiff paper work well because you can act ideas out: Wear the letter *E* as a gladiator's mask or turn it into a flying bird; don the letter *A* as a witch's hat, while cackling, and so on. Your scribe can write down the students' ideas for later transcription if you want. Follow this with one or two short songs or activities.
3. Ask the students questions such as: "What's your favorite food?" "Where were you born?" "What's your favorite season or kind of weather?"
4. Tell the class, "In poetry, we get to visit the magic nation of our imagination. Poetry can also help us see everything as if we'd never seen it before. That's what we were doing when we looked at the alphabet letters in a brand new way."
5. Show them your Magic Bag and have them guess what's inside. It usually takes only a minute before someone says "a poem," and they're right!
6. Tell the students: "We've learned a little about each other. Now, let's see if we can visit the 'magic nation' inside each of us to guess or make believe a little about the objects inside this bag."
7. Pull the objects from the bag one at a time. Play with each one and demonstrate what it can do (you can pass items around if the group is small). Ask the kids to name each one, and squint their eyes: "Look at this in a new way. Use your poet's eyes and tell me what it's like."
8. Return to each object and have the students imagine that *they* are the objects. Ask questions such as: "If you were a whistle, what would you dream about?" "If you were a spoon, where would you dance?" "If you were a candle, who would your mother and father be?" (See the sample poem for more ideas.)
9. The scribe madly writes down all the ideas. (You may have to ask kids to pause while the scribe catches up.)
10. A candle works well as the last object. Rules permitting, light the candle and observe. Then count to three and have the kids blow it out together, then ask, "Where did the flame go?"
11. Read the poem back to the class, stringing the scribe's notes into coherent lines as you pick up each object.
12. Afterward: Type up the scribe's notes into coherent lines and give a copy to the teacher.

Time and Materials: The whole lesson shouldn't be longer than 30 to 40 minutes. The Magic Bag activity is just 10 to 15 minutes. You will need a Magic Bag with 6 to 10 usual and unusual objects inside, and a scribe to write down the students' ideas. Don't forget matches if you use a candle.

Worksheet

If I Was . . . (inspired by objects in a Magic Bag)
  by Mrs. Broderick's Primary-Grade Class, Sonoma County

If I was a magic rain stick
I'd dream about rainy weather.
My best friends would be
another rain stick and a fish in Siberia.

If I was a candle,
I would burn the night.
I'd eat wax, fire and candle food.

If I was an echo bowl,
I'd live in a red house
with pink trim and a green boat
parked out in front—in Israel,
the singing bowl country.

If I was a whistle,
I'd dream about whistling
in someone's ear.
I'd live in a refrigerator
in Santa Rosa.
My favorite foods would be
the sun, red-winged blackbirds,
a rope, and a hawk. I would play music.

If I was a cookie cutter,
I'd go to school in a cookie in Hawaii;
I'd go to school in someone's brain.
My favorite cookies would be
cherry and chocolate cookies.
I'd dream about being a cookie cutter
in cookie cutter school.
I'd be born in the closet.

If I was a spoon,
I would sleep in the silverware drawer.
I would dance at Baskin-Robbins
Thirty-One Flavors.
I would dance in a trash can.
My best friends would be a knife, a fork,
and hands.

Breathe In, Breathe Out
For Grades One Through Five

by Meg Hamill

This lesson plan will appeal to younger writers just learning how to express themselves on the page, as well as older elementary students who are practiced poets. It is a great lesson to use when major events take place in the family, local communities, or around the world, especially those that are tragic or difficult to understand. It will allow young people a way to process events authentically and creatively, and it will also lead to a large number of fantastic poems from all different types of kids—including English-language learners and those who "don't like to write."

1. Bring in a small branch from any tree indigenous to your area. Ask if anyone knows what it is. Use this as an opportunity to teach briefly about a native plant: its name, how indigenous people would have used it, any medicinal properties, and so on.
2. Ask students if they know how trees help human beings to live. (Breathe in carbon dioxide, or CO_2, breathe out oxygen, or O_2.) Make the point that carbon dioxide is harmful for humans to breathe, but oxygen is vital to life.
3. Talk about examples of plants that are able to take in toxins and transform them, such as wetland plants that clean the water by sucking up pollution (or sewage), breaking the toxins down, and changing the pollution into something pure and healthy.
4. Tell the students: "Today we are going to think about human bodies in the same way that we think about trees and wetland plants: as able to transform sad to happy, ugly to beautiful, and so on. Breathing in, we take in something difficult or polluting or bad or painful, and breathing out, we let out something good and healthy and sweet and joyful."
5. Make a chart that looks like a big T on the board and have students copy it on a piece of scratch paper. On one side of the T-chart, put SAD, on the other HAPPY (for younger students) or DIFFICULT/JOYFUL (for older students). You can make up your own headings as well.
6. As a class, come up with a few things for each side of the T-chart, such as: "Tornado," "Death of a family member," and "No rain" for "SAD," and "New baby," "Learning to play guitar," and "Dad found a new job" for "HAPPY." If there has been a recent tragedy or uplifting event that all kids are aware of, be sure to include that on the chart.
7. Now let each child work independently, if age-appropriate, listing three to five (or more) things for each side of their own chart. Remind them that the things on their charts can be very big or very small, personal or global.
8. Pass out and read Judyth Hill's poem "Wage Peace" aloud. You read it once, and then let a student read it out loud. Point out how the poem goes back and forth between "breathe in" and "breathe out."
9. Ask the students about their favorite parts of the poem. Make sure they see that she breathes in difficult things and breathes out lovely things. Then read student examples.
10. Say, "Let's make a poem as a group!" Write a couple of lines of a "Breathe in, breathe out" poem on the board, using suggestions from the students, demonstrating how to extend their thoughts with each line so that their poems move beyond simple list poems.
11. Tell them, "Now it's time for you to write!" Using their T-charts as inspiration (if they wish), have students write poems, reminding them to use the "Breathe in, breathe out" model, repeating those lines as needed.
12. Remind them as they write to use colors, other adjectives, specific names of places, plants, and so on. Big vocabulary charts around the room are helpful. Reading samples of the poems aloud as the kids are writing (with permission) can also spark those who are stuck.

Time and Materials: This lesson will likely take forty-five minutes. You will need a small tree branch and vocabulary posters of colors, flowers, animals, outer space, the five senses, etc.

Worksheet

Wage Peace (September 11, 2001)
by Judyth Hill

Wage peace with your breath.

Breathe in firemen and rubble,
breathe out whole buildings and flocks of red-wing blackbirds.

Breathe in terrorists
and breathe out sleeping children and fresh-mown fields.

Breathe in confusion and breathe out maple trees.

Breathe in the fallen and breathe out lifelong friendships intact.

Wage peace with your listening: hearing sirens, pray loud.

Remember your tools: flower seeds, clothespins, clean rivers.

Make soup.

Play music, memorize the words for thank-you in three languages.

Learn to knit, and make a hat.

Think of chaos as dancing raspberries,
imagine grief
as the outbreath of beauty
or the gesture of fish.

Swim for the other side.

Wage peace.

Never has the world seemed so fresh and precious:

Have a cup of tea and rejoice.

Act as if armistice has already arrived.
Celebrate today.

Breathe In, Breathe Out
by India Buchanan, Taos County, New Mexico

Breathe in people getting hurt,
Breathe out being with my mom.
Breathe in my dad going to war,
Breathe out having play dates.
Breathe in trees getting burned,
Breathe out having picnics.

This Is Life
by Uma Abad, Taos County, New Mexico

I breathe in the death of Venezuela's president,
I breathe out peace.
I breathe in hunger,
I breathe out food for everyone.
I breathe in war,
I breathe out no bullies.
I breathe in thirst,
I breathe out sweet dreams.
I breathe in yucky food,
I breathe out love.

Prompts
I breathe in (something bad, sad, hard), I breathe out (something happy, joyful, peaceful).
What colors would you breathe in and out?
What animals and plants?
What environmental problem/solution?
What kinds of people?
What weather?
What sounds and smells? What types of words?
What emotions? What family problems, solutions?
Extend your thoughts so that your poem does not become a simple list.

Moon Poems For All Ages

by Karen K. Lewis

(Based on a 1995 moon poem project by poet-teachers Terry Ehret and Karin Faulkner.)

In a quest to connect kids to the cycles of nature, one prop is always available: the moon. Visible or invisible, the moon visits our dreams as it changes shape. Mention the phases of the moon and how tribal people through the centuries have named the moon many things: Salmon Moon, Moon When Acorns Scatter, Owl Moon, Snow Moon. This lesson could extend your science unit or stand on its own as a poetry adventure.

1. The day before this lesson, ask your students to notice the night sky and, if possible, to jot down a few words of sounds they hear or things they see at night on a "poetry detective" paper.
2. On poetry day, ask students to share a few words. Write these on the board. Ask students to add to their homework paper with a warm-up list. Categories are flexible: try favorite animal, favorite fruit, something you dream about, a weather word, something that flies. Keep these words secret for now, unless the class is listless, in which case, ask volunteers to share. Any words on the board are then free for anyone to use in their poems. If nobody did their homework, just go with the warm-up lists!
3. Introduce the idea of moon cycles. Ask for examples of what the moon looks like in different phases. Write a few similes on the board. Prompt for unusual ideas. Instead of "a smile," ask "whose smile?"
4. Explain that tribal people have always called the moon different things, based on the seasons. You might share *Thirteen Moons on Turtle's Back* (reading just the titles and showing the illustrations).
5. Ask students to imagine names for the moon the way it is now. Examples might be "Rain Moon," "Moon of Football," "Pumpkin Moon." Prompt them for connections to animals native to your habitat.
6. Read the model poems on the handout. Call attention to line or stanza patterns. Notice that poems are a mixture of real fact and make-believe. (For kindergarten through first grade: Omit the discussion of stanza and line. Create a group moon poem using a scroll on the white board.)
7. Silent writing time: fifteen minutes. Say, "Now we will each write a moon poem." Ask writers to let their imaginations lead them through the writing adventure. I usually dim the lights. If students need help, I guide them to their warm-up words and encourage them to link two words together in a fun, new image. Frog + soccer. Cat + mango, etc. Say, "Do the project your own way. This is a time to discover new things."
8. Remind students to move through the first draft without worrying about spelling. With five minutes remaining, ask them to add details: colors, sounds, an emotion. With two minutes remaining, ask them to make sure their poem ends with a surprise and to create an exciting title.
9. Sharing time: Either form a full-moon circle, or have poets stand and recite their poem in a clear, loud voice. This is the time to celebrate this wild moon that connects us all.

Materials: Small pieces of scrap paper for "Poetry Detective Homework" and/or "Imagination Warm-Ups"; white board with markers; binder paper and pencils. Optional: *Thirteen Moons on Turtle's Back* by Joseph Bruchac; posters that show the scientific phases of the moon; word strips (colorful paper strips that hold your planetary-science vocabulary: *eclipse, lunar, crescent, crater, meteor, star, reflection*, etc.).

Worksheet

Pasajera
  by Alberto Blanco

*La luna es sólo
polvo en las cortinas.*

*Nubes azules
en el espejo del cuarto.*

*Cuando se mira
se pone triste y canta:*

*Su voz conduce
la sombra de los gatos.*

In Passing

The moon is only
dust in the curtains.

Blue clouds
in the mirror of the room.

When she looks at herself
she feels sad and sings:

Her voice guides
a cat's shadow.

(Translated by Judith Infante)

Wolf Moon
  by Allison Lara, Mendocino County

The wolf moon gleams in the night sky.
The wolf moon
is beautiful and white.
The wolf moon
comes every January.
The wolf moon
gives you visions of wolves running.
The wolf moon
is one eye of a white wolf.

Mountain Awakening
  by Jenny Gealy, Mendocino County

    moonrise twice tonight
    first a ripple in the lake
    a giant firefly
    drowning
    then peeking shyly
    over craggy rock
    and snow banks
    white spotlight
    scaring the stars away
    making clouds
    white feathers
    we are tiny now
    drowning in its splendor

(Editor's note: Jenny died in an accident in 1995, the year she wrote this poem.)

In the Center of the Drum (Chant and Rhythm) With Variations for Kindergarten Through Grade Twelve

by Grace Grafton (adapted by Cathy Barber and Phyllis Meshulam)

Goals: To explain and develop the use of rhythm, as exemplified in a chant; to define the form of chant and connect its rhythm with the heartbeat; and to plunge students into the excitement and physicality of poetry by using sound and rhythm as the sensate medium of the poem. In the case of the older kids, we'll emphasize the latter.

1. Beat the drum briefly and introduce yourself as a poet. Ask students to introduce themselves to you. With younger students, you can sit on the floor and beat the drum to repeat each name after the student says it to you, at least for the first few students.
2. Introduce concepts of chant and rhythm. Ask if anyone knows what a *chant* is. A chant, one of the earliest forms of poetry, always uses rhythm, is recited orally (usually by a group), and repeats key phrases. It is ancient, like the drum, the beat of which echoes the heartbeat.
3. Put up a sample poem, recite the poem to the drumbeat, and repeat the poem with the kids, to the drum.
4. Write "In the center of the drum" on the board. Ask what else sounds like the beating of a drum? (What else has a steady rhythm?) What sounds like a flute, a piano, a violin, a trumpet? Write some answers on the board.
5. Write the names of some instruments on the board, along with brief description of their mode of expression, possibly with metaphor ("in the tones of the flute, in the keys of the piano, in the heart of the violin, in the voice of the trumpet") along with some student responses.
6. Explain the exercise: "Write a chant using certain phrases to begin your lines." (Point to phrases on the board.) "Use any of the ideas on the board, add your own ideas, and write about one or all of the instruments, as many lines for each as you want. Try to write at least eight lines. Change anything you want."
7. Dismiss the students to their seats for writing. Distribute paper. Help students individually. Circle the room to make sure everyone is getting started. Repeat the instructions if necessary. *Shhh*, this is quiet time. (With older kids, writing to drum music works.)
8. Fifteen minutes before the end of the lesson, give notice that sharing will begin in two or three minutes, and the students should complete the thought they're on.
9. Collect papers that are finished. Start sharing even if not everyone is done. Call out names. Any student may read, have you read for them, or pass.
10. Share one of your own poems to close, if desired. Congratulate and thank everyone. Get everyone's poem before you leave.
11. Also possible: a chant by the poet-teacher, written for the lesson. Older students, even as young as fourth grade, love the Al Young poem. Many of them really like writing to recorded drum music, translating the beats into words. Students who are very intuitive with this make good tutors to classmates who aren't.

Materials: One of the sample poems, written large on a piece of butcher paper; masking tape or push pins to display the poem in the classroom; a drum, which could be as simple as a can beaten by a pencil. For older students: word charts with onomatopoeia and kinesthetic words; recorded drum music (a 1995 CD called *Abdoul Doumbia*, by the drummer of the same name, works. Track 3 is a good intermediate level of drum music, energetic, but not too wild).

Worksheet

In the Center of the Drum
by Grace Marie Grafton, poet-teacher

In the center of the drum
run animals' feet

In the center of the drum
the thunder rolls

In the center of the drum
the world's heart beats

In the center of the drum
the spirit speaks

Drums of Fury
by Miguel Valadez Licea, Sonoma County

Oh, drums of fury, you make the *kaboom*
   stronger.
You make the rhythm go *beep.*
You make the fury go vengeance.
Anyone can hear you.
Drums, you make the voice in my hand.
Bam boom kaboom.
You are the drums of fury.

Tambores de Furia

Oh tambores de furia,
   que hacéis el cabuuum más fuerte.
Hacéis que el ritmo haga biiip.
Hacéis de la furia venganza.
Quién os escucha tambores
hacéis la voz de mi mano bambuum cabuum.
Vosotros sois los tambores de furia.

(Translated by Fernando Castro, poet-teacher)

Mondo Bongo
by Al Young

Bad drumming always pounds out good,
but badder bongo builds and builds, abounds.
Your everlasting rhythmicness astounds
statues like us who've always understood
you got to get down, down, bippity-bippity down

**Oh, Boom of You, Basketball,
You Make Life**
by Ava Rognlien, Sonoma County

Boom like the wind blows the cold snap of you.
Thunder boom bam dash.
Thunder goes along with the shower of rain.
Both thunder and rain are symphony to my ears.
Clack Cloo Cla.
The heart of my beat goes bowling and
beating, bouncing boom
Heart brings rhythm to my body,
heart of my heart, beating of my life.
The stare of my heart, of my beat,
staring the beat out of me.
A beat, a beat, a beat, a beat, beat,
beat, beat, beat.

Prompts
You can start your poem with one of these lines, if you like:
In the center of the drum . . .
In the tones of the flute . . .
In the keys of the piano. . .
In the heart of the violin . . .
In the voice of the trumpet . . .
Or just let the drum music lead your pencil, using some of the sound words on the board.

The No-Plan Plan
For Kindergarten Through Grade Twelve

by Kathy Evans

One of my favorite lesson plans is to have no lesson plan. In other words, stay present with the kids and what is going on in their lives and in their classrooms. Instead of sample adult poems, which often lead to imitations and take kids out of their own experience and language, just start with the present moment.

I begin with the word today, and I often conclude with "Sometimes I feel like . . ." and have them come up with a simile that best describes how they feel. Or I'll say "If you felt like a color, what color would you be?" I emphasize detail throughout my questions and conversation. "Just give me specifics, not just generalizations," I tell them. The more concrete details, the better.

1. Generate your own set of questions, or use the ones I have put on the worksheet. But as you ask the questions out loud with the class, write the answers down (or have the teacher do it on chart paper or on the board) beginning with "Today" or "Right now." This technique gets you immediately into the world of the kids' level of thinking and perceiving instead of yours. Then just listen. Honor what is spoken. This line of casual inquiry and "scribing" is great for generating interest and energy. It is a way of tuning in.

2. As you are writing kids' answers, take the opportunity to demonstrate the difference between specific details and generalized language, close-up details, and faraway details. For example, you point out that there is a difference between the words *candy*, or more exact, *red licorice, Now & Laters*, or *Big Hunks*; a difference between *baked goods*, or *plump, glazed donuts* and *cinnamon buns; the beach* or *Stinson Beach; New York* or *the New York subway, El train; flowers* or *black-eyed Susans* and *sprigs of lilacs; lightning* or *lightning bug*.

3. After the warm-up, each child is then given a questionnaire, and he or she responds to it individually. I hand out special pencils for those who come up with the best and most specific list.

4. The students' lists may be their poem.

5. Or you can collect their individual questions and answers and weave together a group poem for the next week. Bring it in on a big sheet of paper and hang it up.

Note: The sample poem is from Jaishyne, age nine, at the time a patient at the Benioff Children's Hospital, where Sally Doyle and I provide poetry writing sessions every Thursday to kids in the cancer ward. Jaishyne loved writing poetry. No matter how sick he was or how many IVs he had in his arm, he wanted to write or, on certain days, dictate his ideas. His poem is a wonderful expression of his human spirit and resilience.

Materials: Worksheet, board or chart paper, writing supplies.

Worksheet

Questionnaire
- Today, what did you see on the way to school? Name an object, a specific something in the natural world.
- Where you are now?
- What is going on in your head right now? What are you thinking about?
- When your mind wanders, what do you wonder about?
- What happened yesterday? In a few days what is going to happen?
- What is the most important thing to you at the moment? Today? Right now? Be honest. I won't tell anybody.
- What are you learning in school that has you puzzled, or excited?
- What is it that you can't wait for?
- What makes you sad, or happy?
- Give me three of your spelling words or terms from something you are studying.
- What are you reading?
- What is going on in the world right now, today, that you know about?
- What is your favorite activity?
- What do you like to do at recess? What do you touch or hear on the playground?

Jaishyne's Thoughts
  Jaishyne Lopez, San Joaquin County

Today I am thinking about Bingo.
I am thinking about the prizes and toys I'm going to win
like a Lego set. Today
I would like to go to Mars. I would walk around
in my space helmet and my blue space suit and I would carve
Andre's face on the planet. I would look around for life.
Today I am thinking about my family.
They are having seafood in Stockton.
They are thinking about me.
Right now I am feeling happy
because I am about to beat the next level on the video game.
Today there is a book on the shelf that is talking to me, saying "Read Me!"
Today Neptune is on my mind. I want thirty moons on Neptune.
On Thursday I will turn into Spiderman.
Sometimes I feel sad as rain when I get poked by needles,
but then I feel like a new color rising up to slither around.

Poems on Poems (*Ars Poetica*: The Art of Poetry) For Kindergarten Through Grade Twelve

by Julie Hochfeld

"*Dulce et utile*": poetry must be both "sweet and useful." Horace gave this advice in 19 BCE in a famous 476-line poem later entitled "Ars Poetica." While Horace's poem instructs writers, the *ars poetica* form has since expanded to include many kinds of poems about poetry. Best done later in a residency after reading and writing numerous poems, the *ars poetica* lesson gives students an opportunity to celebrate the art of poetry while playing with imagination, similes, metaphors, and personification. What better way to honor art than to create more art! Both useful and sweet . . .

1. Discuss the idea of *ars poetica*, "the art of poetry" in Latin, and Horace's advice to make poetry "*dulce et utile*," both sweet and useful. Tell students they will be using their imaginations to write poems about poetry.
2. Read the sample poems aloud. Students can take turns reading, or if they are young, the teacher and/or poet-teacher can read.
3. You can discuss all or some of the sample poems. For instance, what do students think Gary Snyder compares poetry to? What could they compare poetry to? And/or discuss the patterns in "Where Poetry Comes From" and the use of metaphors in "Ars Poetica."
4. You can write these prompts on the board and read them aloud (see the abbreviated version on the next page): Poetry is . . . Poetry came from . . . How poetry comes . . . Who stole poetry? Who gave poetry? Where/how to find poetry? What poetry wants is . . . Who is a poet? Where does poetry hide? Where was poetry lost? Who found poetry? Where or when has poetry been forgotten? Where did poetry go? Where does poetry live? How does poetry look, smell, taste, sound, feel? Be specific. Use the five senses.
5. There are several ways to proceed: (a) the class can write a group poem; (b) the class can write a group poem and then individual poems, either during this session or the next; or (c) you can move directly to individual writing.
6. If you begin with a group poem, have the class brainstorm about five ideas, then vote on one. Group poems are great for emerging writers and/or students with lesser skills. But if you have limited time and capable writers, go directly to individual writing. You can still write brainstormed ideas on the board to get ideas flowing. And then write, write, write!
7. When the writing period is over, share the poems. If there is time, classmates can give at least one specific, positive comment for each poem.
8. Many *ars poetica* poems are available online, which, depending on the grade level, might enrich your lesson. Examples include "How to Eat a Poem," by Eve Merriam; "Valentine for Ernest Mann," by Naomi Shihab Nye; "Poetry," by Pablo Neruda; "Ars Poetica," by Archibald MacLeish; "Eating Poetry," by Mark Strand; and "How to Read a Poem," by Pamela Spiro Wagner. Poets.org and other sites have many more *ars poetica* poems.
9. I believe in the power of samples. Each time you teach this lesson, you can save strong samples. Teach poems *you* like that approach the same theme in a variety of ways.

Time : The lesson will take forty-five to sixty minutes. It will take longer if students write both group and individual poems.

Worksheet

How Poetry Comes to Me
by Gary Snyder

It comes blundering over the
Boulders at night, it stays
Frightened outside the
Range of my campfire
I go to meet it at the
Edge of the light

Where Poetry Comes From
by Julie Hochfeld, poet-teacher

Poetry washed ashore high tide,
a white shell in smooth, fine sands.

Poetry drifted like petals
and landed in a child's hands.

Poetry grew in spring gardens,
bright flowers covered in dew.

Poetry traveled sea and land;
it swam, it walked, and it flew.

Poetry bloomed in deep silence;
unfurled its blossoms in sound.

Poetry spread in the compost
and made a maze underground.

Poetry rose from dying breaths
and from women giving birth.

Poetry painted autumn leaves,
rich colors blessing the earth.

Poetry was stirred into soup
and poured into waiting bowls.

Poetry sings in each new child
and brings us back to our souls.

Ars Poetica
by Maygan Graves, Humboldt County

Poetry is the dewdrops
    on my window in the early morning.
Poetry is forgiving. You can put
    anything down on the page.
Poetry is the jellyfish
    who are so graceful in the ocean.
Poetry can transform
    into whatever you want it to.
Poetry is a pinkish orangish
    rose that is coming to life.
Poetry is the sound of people
    on the street playing music.
Poetry is inside everyone.
    You just have to look harder.

**Trees Teach Poetry
and Teachers Teach Me**
by Kehlan Ballew, Humboldt County

Poetry comes from teachers.
Some teachers are nice.
Teachers get the poetry from trees.
The trees sing the poetry
and the teachers hear it.
The teachers ask the trees
if they can learn the songs.
The trees say,
"Make sure to listen real well."
And the teachers say,
"Bye, thank you!
We'll for sure
teach it to the children."

Prompts

Poetry is … Poetry came from … Who stole/gave poetry? Where/how to find poetry? Poetry wants/hides/lives … Who is a poet? Where was poetry lost? Who found poetry? Where/when has poetry been forgotten? How does poetry look, smell, taste, sound, feel?

Use the five senses! Be specific! Have fun!

Mostly in the Middle

Secret Place
For Grades Three Through Six

by Perie Longo

When my daughter Cecily was in third grade, the mother of one of her friends asked why I taught young children poetry. I found myself saying, to discover their inner life, their "secret place," so to speak. Coincidentally, my daughter and I had just finished reading *The Secret Garden* by Frances H. Burnett. In the chapter titled "Magic," Colin says, "everything is made out of magic; leaves and trees, flowers and birds, badgers and foxes and squirrels and people. . . . Magic is in me." All children believe this, and especially sense it when free to explore their world. They just don't talk about it until given the opportunity.

1. To introduce the lesson, ask who has read or seen *The Secret Garden*. Read the above quote. Ask how many of them have a secret place they like to go to when they are alone or with a special friend. Places begin to emerge: creeks, trees, forts, bedrooms, mountaintops, beaches, a cave in the woods.
2. You might also ask how many travel to places in their imagination.
3. You might read from D. H. Lawrence's poem "Delight of Being Alone." He writes, "It makes me realise the delicious pleasure of the moon / that she has in travelling by herself: throughout time . . ." Ask what the students like about being alone.
4. Read the sample poem "My Secret Place." Ask students if they can guess where the place might be and what gives them a clue.
5. Ask a student to read it, then ask the class which lines or phrases they like. Do they spot any similes? Descriptions? Is there anything they don't understand?
6. What happens in the poem that is unusual? Is there something that feels magical?
7. What do they think the poet means when she says, "Weather can't make up its mind / in my secret place?" Discuss what the words *sunshade*, *brightrain*, and *moonbows* might be saying. You could mention that the poet e. e. cummings often ran words together and that poets like to make up words.
8. What do they think the poet is talking about when she says, "Shhhh / Sheep are being counted." You might mention that writing a poem can feel a little like sleeping.
9. Read "Secret Place" by Cecily Longo. Ask the students what images make her place special. Do they hear any words that sound good together? Read the second poem by Jake as example of an "imaginary place" and discuss similar points. Is there anything magical or special about either of their places?
10. List on the board some questions the students can think about when writing their poem. What does their secret place look like? What do they see, hear, and feel there? Does anything unusual or magic happen there? Does a friend come along?
11. It's always good to play soft music. Allow ten to fifteen minutes for writing time. Help those who are feeling "stuck" by pointing to the questions.
12. Give the students as much time as possible for sharing their poems.

Time and Materials: One hour for writing and sharing. You will need small, colored index cards cut in half with words printed on them: everyday nouns and verbs from poems or anywhere, really. Students can dip their hands in a paper bag and pick out a few (five or six at most). Words are like magic. One can remind us of hundreds of others, opening up a whole new thought or feeling or pricking the imagination.

Worksheet

My Secret Place
by Perie Longo, poet-teacher

My secret place is full
of cat whiskers and a snake skin
smooth as water with diamonds on its back blazing
like freshly packed snowballs
I bat to the sun
which whistles them down
as poems shouting
        Let me out
        Hurl me around the world
        For everyone to hear

Weather can't make up its mind
in my secret place
full of sunshade
           brightrain
                moonbows
and child hushes piping music
through pencils   Shhhhhh
Sheep are being counted

My Imaginary Football Field
by Jake Knecht, Santa Barbara County

I go when I have nothing else to do.
I ride my bike down there
and pretend there are players running
at me to give me a hug.
I spend almost the whole day there.
I can hear the crowd going wild
when I score a touchdown,
even when I'm pretending.
My favorite time to go there is when
it is raining. I get muddy as a dog
playing in the mud. I play until
it gets dark and I can't see anything
and nobody knows about it.

Secret Place
by Cecily Longo, Santa Barbara County

My secret place
is where bamboo is crisp

Wind whips the tall trees
in twists and turns

Trees grow in creeks
while leaves spin their destiny

Mud banks are cozy and warm
My secret place stays the same
      in a storm

Prompts
Describe what your secret place looks like.
What do you see, hear, and feel there?
Does anything unusual or magic happen there?
Does a friend come along?

California Poets In The Schools

The Shy Sky (Personification) For Grades Four Through Six

by Gail Newman

I always start my workshops with a series of lessons about figurative language, or the special language tools of poetry. We talk about how poets use words in surprising ways, often not literal but evocative and visual. Personification creates strong sensory images and helps us see the world come alive. This lesson can stand alone or be introduced at any point in a poetry-writing unit.

1. Ask: "What words could you use to describe the sky?" Examples might be *blue, cloudy, high*.
2. Say: "What if I said, 'shy sky?' What kind of sky and what kind of day might that be?"
3. Ask: "How does the sky seem to feel on a cloudy day? Does it make you feel the same way? Do you think the sky REALLY feels those emotions?"
4. "Have you ever noticed how the branches of a tree seem to reach out like human hands to touch the sky? What do they seem to be trying to do? There's a special word we use when we imagine that things have human qualities."
5. Write on the board: *Personification.*
6. Say: "Let's read the word *personification* together." (Repeat the word together.) Ask: "What word do you see hiding in this big word?" (person).
7. "Today we're going to practice personification. Let's look at some poems that use this tool."
8. Read "Walking Beside a Creek" by Ted Kooser, a poet who often uses personification in his poems. Tell the students that this poet lives in Nebraska and received the Pulitzer Prize (explain) in 2005 for his book *Delights and Shadows*. You may want to add that Kooser worked as an insurance agent for many years. Lots of poets have jobs besides writing! He said, "What would be wrong with a world in which everyone were writing poems?" With older kids, you may choose to read "In an Old Apple Orchard," or both poems.
9. Ask: "Where do you notice personification in this poem?" Discuss: "How do the trees feel? What are they wearing? Why? What kind of day is it? Which part of the tree might be the boots? What might they be wearing in the summer?"
10. Ask: "Why might a poet use personification?" (For example: to establish a mood or to create an image that helps the reader see more clearly.)
11. Look at a photo of a tree together and brainstorm words to describe it. Write on board.

    Example: a picture of a tree **Sample Answers:**
    - What part of a *human body* does it look like? *The branches hold up the sky.*
    - What does it seem to do that a person *does*? *Listen to the wind whisper secrets.*
    - What human *feeling* might it have? *Why so sad today in the storm,*
    - What does it seem to *wear*? *dressed in dry brown leaves?*
    - What is the *human quality*? *Standing tall and proud in the rain.*

12. Say: "Today you can use pictures to inspire a poem using personification."
13. Tell the students: "Here are two poems written by kids your age who were looking at pictures of nature." Read the poems by Hannah and Ronin.
14. Pass out nature photos. Ask the children to choose one.
15. Ask: "Does anyone have a question? Okay. Now ten minutes of quiet time. Go."
16. Write. Share.

Materials: A photo of a tree, plus animal photos or other nature pictures (from magazines, calendars, the Internet), a list or cards with verbs: things people do, such as *read, sew, sleep, wash, kneel, cook, build*. Note: For younger grades, ask the children to focus on just one quality, such as movement. For example: "What do things in nature do?" *Grow, blow, wilt, shake, break . . .*

Worksheet

Walking Beside a Creek
by Ted Kooser

Walking beside a creek
in December, the black ice
windy with leaves,
you can feel the great joy
of the trees, their coats
thrown open like drunken men,
the lifeblood thudding
in their tight, wet boots.

In an Old Apple Orchard
by Ted Kooser

The wind's an old man
to this orchard; these trees
have been feeling
the soft tug of his gloves
for a hundred years.
Now it's April again,
and again that old fool
thinks he's young.
He's combed the dead leaves
out of his beard; he's put on
perfume. He's gone off
late in the day
toward the town, and come back
slow in the morning,
reeling with bees.
As late as noon, if you look
in the long grass,
you can see him
still rolling about in his sleep.

The Trees Play
by Hannah Urisman, San Francisco County

The trees play with the smooth
knowledge of happiness.
They gather the fragile dreams
of poetry.
They become overjoyed
with the freedom of the sun.
They run far to the land of memory
and music.
They stand tall with their legs
made of rumbling beauty.
They wait until the flowers die
to whisper secrets to each other.

The Desert Life and Rhythm
by Ronin Mukai, San Francisco County

The desert is as dry and cracked
as an old man's heel.

The desert chews up life.

If you search deep in the desert
you'll find it delightful.

The answer is a rhyme of
life and death.

Advice to Writers

Personification is one of many poetry tools, a way of seeing the world. It's not cartoony or surreal, but a metaphor for how *things* sometimes seem to act like *people*.

Prompts (looking at your picture)

What part of a human *body* does it look like?
What does it seem to do that a person *does*?
What human *feeling* might it have?
What does it seem to *wear*?
What is the human *quality*?

California Poets In The Schools

Grand Slam Poetry (Hyperbole) For Grades Two Through Eight

by Susan Terence

When I saw a sea of orange and black T-shirts and baseball caps on the fourth-graders in Jim Dwyer's class at Commodore Sloat Elementary School in San Francisco, I knew that for our next lesson we had to honor and combine two traditions that San Francisco is famous for: baseball and poetry. You can make this lesson work either at the time of spring training or when the World Series draws near.

1. Compile and print out a glossary of baseball terms and equipment: *pitcher, catcher, batter, outfielder, first base, second base, third base, shortstop, home plate, foul ball, strike, walk, hit, run, fly ball, safe, umpire, coach, manager, error, home run, fair ball, glove, bat, baseball.*

2. Print out the roster of a nearby Major League Baseball team.

3. Using hyperbole is perfect for this poetry lesson, as students' descriptions of their favorite baseball team or player are often "larger than life." The concept of exaggerating or naming something impossible is very appealing to young children in their writing.

4. Using the equipment mentioned below, let students take turns enacting simple baseball terms from the vocabulary list—*walk, strike, foul, fly, home run, stealing a base, bunt,* and *error*—in slow motion, though, so as not to cause any damage in the classroom!

5. Have older students (grades three through eight) read aloud and enact Ernest Thayer's "Casey at the Bat" (using the plastic bat). When students finish reenacting the poem, they often say, "It was a sad poem. It has a bad ending." Discuss.

6. Have class read aloud the other sample poems.

7. Compose a group poem in which students are first asked to consider the ambiance of the baseball stadium: the wet night air, spilled popcorn, peanuts, and Cracker Jacks, sounds of bats cracking, the earthquake-intensity foot-stomping of the crowds, and the sheer beauty of a baseball flying into the night sky.

8. Students then compose their own poems using the glossary of baseball terms and a vocabulary list like this one: *sticky, slippery, wet, bases, baseball diamond, stadium, field, grass, dugout, cap, cleats, bobblehead, throwing, pitching, spinning, hurling, tossing, catching, batting, hitting, slugging, swinging, walking, running, flying, gliding, sliding, sour, salty, steaming, sizzling, hot dogs, peanuts, Cracker Jacks, sky, cloud, star, moon, sun, hooting, hollering, yelling, excitement, joy, ecstasy, fear, fury, anger, sadness, quiet, calm, peace, craziness, silliness, wishes, dreams, hopes, sun, moon, stars, comet, galaxy, spring, summer, autumn, twilight, midnight, afternoon.*

Materials: Plastic bat, ball, hat, mitt, baseball glossary, the complete poem of "Casey at the Bat," printed from the Internet.

Worksheet

Wild as the Wind
by Flora Chen, San Francisco County

I am the autumn wind
cooling everyone
in the stands.
I'm the silver sky
of the bat
ready to hit.
I'm the stadium at noon
when everything's
as wild as the wind.

Looking at the Night Sky
by Daniel Doan, San Francisco County

It's a silver bat hitting a blue baseball
in the night sky while wolves awake
in hidden caves near the calm
Pacific Ocean filled with creatures
looking at the night sky
like the icy Milky Way
while scientists seek new planets.

It's a Blue Meteor Falling
by Alex Intara, San Francisco County

It's stars bursting on top of second base.
Baseball of thunder roaring.
Baseball of foggy nights.
It's the umpire yelling a foul.
It's a blue meteor falling.

The Stadium at Midnight
by Jocelyn Tran, San Francisco County

I wish I were a shiny golden
bat hitting the baseball
high over the moon.
I wish I were a smooth
silver baseball
soaring in the sky.
I wish I were
the stadium at midnight
quiet as a mouse.

It's Magic!
by Raymond Vallee, San Francisco County

It's magic in the
crazy loud Giants
Stadium when Juan Uribe
whacks the red and white
baseball into the blue
waters of McCovey's Cove

Casey at the Bat—(last two stanzas)
by Ernest Lawrence Thayer

… The sneer is gone from Casey's lip, his teeth are clenched in hate,
He pounds with cruel violence his bat upon the plate;
And now the pitcher holds the ball, and now he lets it go,
And now the air is shattered by the force of Casey's blow.

Oh, somewhere in this favoured land the sun is shining bright,
The band is playing somewhere, and somewhere hearts are light;
And somewhere men are laughing, and somewhere children shout,
But there is no joy in Mudville—mighty Casey has struck out.

Prompts
- "I wish I were . . ." "It's the . . ." "Fields of . . ." "Baseball of . . ." "Stadium of . . ." "I'm the . . ." "Inside . . ."
- Use at least two metaphors, colors, textures, sounds, flavors, actions, sky words, places, baseball terms, emotions, and hyperbole.

Apples to Apples (Juxtaposition) For All Ages
(A super-fun exercise that helps all writers find specific and surprising images inside abstract ideas)

by Michelle Bitting

I love the game Apples to Apples, and most people I know, adults and children alike, do too! A huge part of why I love it is the way it gets the mind leaping in unusual directions. It allows the player to associate a random description with a wild noun that the imagination might not normally make. During a series of writing workshops on finding concrete imagery inside "big" ideas and feelings, I always find some time to play this with the class as a group brainstorming "game." It serves as a provocative lead-in to their personal writing time. The results are often hilarious and shocking—the writers always get limbered and amped to write—the pencils fly to the page!

1. Open your bright red Apples to Apples game box. Look through the green adjective cards. Pick five or so that feel particularly compelling. Don't think too hard about it. For instance, just now I pulled out *savage, majestic, heroic, nauseating,* and *classy.*

2. Pass out the red noun cards, face down, one or two to each student. (If you are doing this exercise on your own, you can "deal" yourself more: ten to twenty at least would make sense.)

3. Write the five green-card words on the board, allowing enough room beneath each one for a list of phrases. (Again, if you are by yourself, you can make columns on a piece of paper.)

4. Now, instruct the students to turn their cards over and think about which adjective they'd match their nouns with. As the poets share their nouns, write them down under the adjective column they've chosen. Some students will be wild in their associations, while others choose more logical pairings. Both are great! There is no right or wrong.

5. As you build the columns, you can subtly discuss why some pairings work well even when they are strange, and yet there is a point where extreme or too absurd can go too far and it's not as effective. Why is that? Art is mysterious, isn't it?

6. Read the sample poems. What images do the kids like? Have the kids pick one of the abstract words from the worksheet.

7. It's time to write solo! Now, have students make lists of images and phrases they connect with that chosen word. Tell them: "Be specific, very 'concrete'; be daring and wild!" Suddenly they will have "heroic gym lockers," "majestic meat grinders," "savage wonders of the world"—who knows where the list might go and what poems might arise!

8. From there they can develop their list into longer lines or even a narrative-type poem.

Time and Materials: One shiny red box of the Apples to Apples game, Junior for younger school age children, and Regular for teens and adults. You can sort through the green and red cards and toss aside any nouns that feel too obscure or inappropriate, for whatever reason. There are plenty to spare!

Worksheet

Loneliness
 by Daisy Robertson, Los Angeles County

Loneliness is a flower with no petals,
a pen with no ink to talk to, a dark
room with nothing in it. Loneliness
is a crayon box with only one crayon,
the color white, so blank and plain.

Beauty
 by Charles Baudelaire

I am beautiful, oh mortals! like a dream of stone
And my breast, where every one of you is ravaged in turn,
Is made to inspire the poet with
Eternal and mute love, as well as material.

I sit enthroned in azure like a misunderstood sphinx;
I unite a heart of snow with the whiteness of swans;
I hate movement that shifts the lines,
And I never cry nor do I laugh.

Poets, confronted with my lofty airs,
Which I appear to borrow from the proudest monuments,
Will consume their days in austere study;

For, to fascinate these docile lovers,
I have pure mirrors that make everything more beautiful;
My eyes, my wide eyes, eternally bright!

(Translated by Paula Koneazny)

Funny!
 by Bella Rahi, Los Angeles County

Funny is a weird silence in the classroom
or you being you while riding
a unicycle. Funny is like strolling along
spaghetti lane with butter in your toes
and meatballs in your hair on your way to school.
Funny is like being happy not sad.
Funny is a good thing to feel—always feel!

Advice to Writers

The beauty of this exercise is that it so immediately allows your mind and imagination to let go and take chances. Choose a big, juicy abstraction like *Love, Courage, Loneliness, Death, Boredom or Grief, Peace, Beauty, Fear, Happiness.* Now make lists of images and phrases you connect with that chosen word—be specific, very "concrete"—be daring and wild! From there you can develop your list into longer lines or even a narrative-type poem. Let your mind amaze you!

Sensing the Way Home: Using Maps to Remember Every Detail For Grades Three Through Five

by Susan Sibbet (adapted by Cathy Barber)

I love this exercise because the student poems always surprise me, filled as they are with kitchens and closets, and secret treasure waiting for us to find it.

1. Begin with the question: "How do you know where you are?" Maps and GPS may come up in the discussion!
2. Show the students maps and books about maps. I like *You Are Here: Personal Geographies and Other Maps of the Imagination* by Katharine Harmon and, for the younger students, *My Map Book* by children's illustrator Sara Fanelli, but any maps would be good. Suggest to the students that they can map anything: their bedroom, street, house, stomach, heart.
3. On the board, write some words from the special vocabulary of mapmakers. You can explain as necessary for the particular class. Some possibilities: s*cale, four directions, compass rose, legend, atlas, key, floor plan, cross-section.*
4. Sketch a floor plan on the board of a place they all know: the school, the classroom or the playground. Ask them to help you fill in the details. Where does the teacher's desk go? Where are the monkey bars? The water fountain?
5. Then add some sensory details: What noise does the pencil sharpener make? Do the trees have a smell? Remember we have five senses! Use a few!
6. Show a dollhouse or a picture of a cross-section of an apartment building or house. Do you think about a place differently when you see it as a cross-section?
7. Ask students to think of a place they want to discover with imagination: a favorite place, like their own house, or a hiding place where they keep secrets, and tell them that in a few minutes we will write poems about our imagined places.
8. Read Francisco X. Alarcón's "La Misión" as an example of a poem about a place. Point out some of the details in Alarcón's poem and remind students that details, especially sensory details, will help their poems come alive. Ask one of the students to read "My Road Back Home," by student Vincent "Burtsie" Maruffo and ask the students to point out some sensory details in this poem, too.
9. Now, it is time to write! Give the students a few more things to think about as they are about to write: Is there a door to their imaginary place? a tunnel? What will it sound like in their room/cave/heart? Will there be smells to follow? Is their place cold or comfortable, far or near?
10. Give the students at least ten minutes to write or until it feels as if they are done.
11. Leave time for students to read their poems, and ask the other students what they notice in each classmate's poem.

Materials: Maps. Optional: The books *You Are Here: Personal Geographies and Other Maps of the Imagination* by Katharine Harmon and *My Map Book* by Sara Fanelli; a dollhouse or a picture of a cross-section of a building; diagrams of the heart, the brain, the ocean—all with labels.

Worksheet

La Misión
San Francisco
  by Francisco X. Alarcón

buenos días
colores
vida mía

buenas tardes
risas
pan de olor

cómo están
gente
mitotera

puertas tristes
música
de ventanas

caras jóvenes
riqueza
de los más pobres

un día
yo puedo dejar
el barrio

pero éste
nunca saldrá
de mí

The Mission
San Francisco
  by Francisco X. Alarcón

good morning
colors
life of mine

good afternoon
laughter
fragrant bread

what's new
people
the latest gossip

sad doors
music
from windows

young faces
riches
of the very poor

one day
I may leave
this place

but *el barrio*
will never
leave me

My Road Back Home
  by Vincent "Burtsie" Maruffo,
  Mendocino County

If I follow this road
back home
I walk through
thick black shadows
alone
through late October mist
moonlight in front
imagining the wet grass
smells of morning
the early bird songs
promising to chirp
for the meaning of a new day
telling me
I will make it
back home
for the moon
won't leave me
alone

Prompts

If I follow…
Good morning (night), _____
I enter a door … a tunnel…
I follow the smell of…
I feel cold…comfortable…
It is far from…
It is near…

Use your senses and collect all those details!

California Poets In The Schools

Making a Poem Hum: Combining Alliteration with Onomatopoeia For Grades Three Through Six

by Terri Glass

I love reading poems aloud that use alliteration and onomatopoeia imaginatively. They are fun for the mouth to say and for the ear to hear. I often teach this as the third lesson in a series of five, after students have learned metaphor and simile. They'll be able to make a compact poem combining sound and image.

1. Begin by explaining that alliteration, one of our poetry tools for the day, is like a tongue twister: beginning sounds are repeated over and over. Ask if any student knows a tongue twister. Examples: *Peter Piper picked a peck of pickled peppers. Sally sold seashells by the seashore.* What sounds are repeated?
2. Alliteration is usually a little subtler in a poem. In poetry, repeating the beginning sounds of words close together may happen only in two words in a line, and may be scattered in different places in a poem. Alliteration makes sound roll off the tongue and is very pleasant for the ear to hear.
3. Ask the students to create an alliteration in front of their name. Examples: Terrific Terri, Awesome Amanda, Wacky Will.
4. Next, introduce *onomatopoeia:* naming a thing or action by vocal imitation.
5. Ask the students to be totally quiet for two minutes. What sounds did they hear? Can the students name them? Breathing, tapping, humming, coughing, and so on. List them on the board. Many of these words sound a lot like what they mean. Tap your pencil and compare the sound to the word *tap*.
6. You may also ask what different sounds a dog makes and list those on the board for examples: *whine, yelp, woof, bark, pant, growl*. Tell students the English language is full of onomatopoeic words that make sound come alive instantly to the reader or listener.
7. Read three to four poems from Douglas Florian's books *insectlopedia* and *on the wing,* which have excellent examples of using both alliteration and onomatopoeia inside a poem. His books are also cleverly illustrated. You can also share the student poems on the worksheet.
8. Have students find the onomatopoeic words first. Ask: What sounds do the creatures make? Where is there alliteration? Are the words back to back or within a line? Are any metaphors or similes being used?
9. Next, replicate the following chart on the board, on chart paper, or with a projector. It gives examples of these devices to aid students in creating a compact poem about a creature that makes sound. You can use this chart to create some examples.

Alliteration	Creature	Metaphor/Simile	Onomatopoeia	Action
hungry	hummingbird	helicopter	hum	hovers
daring	dragonfly	blue as topaz	whooshes	flying
angry	alligator	mean machine	chomps	swims

10. Ask the children to think about an animal that makes sound and what it may do in the course of a day. Then the students will compose a short poem with three to four alliterations scattered throughout the poem, and one to two onomatopoeic sounds: one the animal makes or what it might hear. Add one simile about what the animal looks like, or what action it may have. Note: A student may include more than one animal in a poem that focuses on place.

Time and Materials: Fifty to sixty minutes. You will need a white board, a document reader, chart paper, or an overhead projector to create the lists and chart. Optional: Douglas Florian's books *insectlopedia* and *on the wing* add a lot.

Worksheet

by Douglas Florian

Barely bigger than your thumb,
See it hover, hear it hum,
With beating wings so fast they're blurred,
This helicopter of a bird.

The Monkeys
   by Mariella Todebush, Marin County

Through green and screeching noise
swing the furry monkeys.
They pick ticks out of their tangled wirehair
munch chew eating bananas and bugs
launch through trees like little fleas
climb tall in the world of leaves.
How I wish to swing and sway
like those little monkeys.

In the Land of Snow
   by Isaiah McGrue, Marin County

In the land of snow,
icicles dance
and rest upon the polar bear's nose.
The narwhal circles icebergs
splish-splash-spray
SLAM!
There goes a polar bear.
The winded white rabbit
with coat smooth as silk,
feet pit pat
against the icy ground.
Mountaintops hover all dusted in white,
patches of green
peek from their ivory blanket.
Icicles dance
in the land of snow.

Advice to Writers
This poem does not have to be long. It can be compact and still be full of interesting sounds. Think about the action of the animal first and what it looks like. The animal may make a sound with its mouth or its body to create the onomatopoeia. Make up an onomatopoeic word, if you wish! The alliterations can go in front of any noun as an adjective, or after a noun as a verb, and can be added later. Sprinkle them throughout the poem.

On the Other Side of . . . (Repetition and Concrete Details) For Grades Three Through Six

by Cathy Barber (adapted from Perie Longo's original lesson)

This lesson analyzes sample poems for tone and concrete images, and encourages students to write poems using repetition and concrete details. Students can use their imagination to create a fantasy or use the opportunity to explore a serious subject, emotion, or concept.

1. Start by passing out the worksheet with the sample poems.
2. Read Perie's poem aloud, then talk a bit about the poem. Ask: "What purpose does the repetition of 'On the other side of the field' serve? Do you feel like you are there each time Perie uses that phrase? Is it like she is actually remembering or looking out her window? What are the images of nature in the poem (rabbits, coyotes, oak trees, weeds, etc.)? Can you see the rabbits? The eucalyptus grove?" Talk about how specific images help the reader see exactly what the poet wanted him or her to see. And what about those students? How does Perie feel about her students? And the tadpoles? Ask what the tadpoles have to do with the students. In other words, unpack the poem and look at its parts carefully. (Perie suggests abbreviating her poem for younger students.)
3. Ask for five volunteers to each read one stanza of Korn's poem, gently helping with any pronunciation problems so the reading is fairly fluid. Look at all the images and details, many of them from nature, as in Perie's poem. Talk about tone: Is this a happy poem? a sad poem? What about Perie's poem? Does it have the same tone?
4. Ask for a student volunteer to read Sarah's poem. Say a few words about what a good poem it is, but that we won't discuss it now because it is almost time to write.
5. Tell the students that they are going to write their own "On the Other Side of" poems. You have already read about the other side of a field, a poem, tomorrow. What else could the students explore? Brainstorm some ideas and write them on the board to help to expand their ideas from the list below or others. Make sure there are a few time options and a few that allow for internal exploration. Remind the students to use images so the reader will see what they see, and suggest that they might want to use a repeating phrase in their poems. Suggest that they think about what used to be "on the other side of . . ." but no longer is. What remains in their memory of what was?
6. Allow the students to write for about ten minutes or until it seems they are done.
7. Ask for volunteers to read their poems. No one is made to read if they don't want to, but usually almost all the students want to read. Stay at the front of the class with each student as he or she reads. Ask the other students to name one thing they noticed in the reader's poem. This happens very quickly; don't linger on the details.

Time and Materials: About one hour. A copy of the following prompts on the board, on chart paper, or ready to be projected.

Prompts

On the other side of . . .

- the window
- the schoolyard
- the fence
- when you were little
- the world
- time
- the year/month/day
- my confidence/failure/hopes
- the moon
- my sadness
- a coin/book/hat
- darkness
- the forest/ocean/river/street
- my face/eyes
- that hill/door/house/field
- space

Worksheet

On the Other Side of the Poem
 by Rachel H. Korn

On the other side of the poem there is an orchard,
and in the orchard, a house with a roof of straw,
and three pine trees,
three watchmen who never speak, standing guard.

On the other side of the poem there is a bird,
yellow brown with a red breast,
and every winter he returns
and hangs like a bud in the naked bush.

On the other side of the poem there is a path
as thin as a hairline cut,
and someone lost in time
is treading the path barefoot, without a sound.

On the other side of the poem amazing things may happen,
even on this overcast day,
this wounded hour
that breathes its fevered longing in the windowpane.

On the other side of the poem my mother may appear
and stand in the doorway awhile lost in thought,
then call me home as she used to call me home long ago,
You've played enough, Rachel. Don't you see? It's night.

(Translated from the Yiddish by Seymour Levitan)

Tomorrow
  by Sarah Stretch, San Mateo County

On the other side of tomorrow
amazing things are happening.
On the other side of tomorrow,
yesterday happens again.

On the other side of tomorrow,
the sun is shining,
children run through a bright, mossy
    forest.
On the other side of tomorrow,
little children's grandpas don't die.

On the other side of tomorrow,
rainbows stretch across the world,
the wet fog is gone,
leaving only a clear day.

The Field Out Back
(for my young poetry students)
 by Perie Longo, poet-teacher

On the other side of the field behind
our house, rabbits are running for cover,
young coyotes cry for their parents—
I come eye to eye with one,
offer it some bread, but it runs from me
as all wild things do, me with the smell
of enemy, of flesh. Me who wants
the best for anyone near or far.

This poem wants to hold them, build
burrows and caves with extra covers
thrown over the old redwood table
under the tangerine tree. On the other side
of the field once there were weeds
so high they hid my favorite oak
on the farthest hill, where I used to walk
with my children, exploring animal tracks
on Sunday between pancakes and typing
your poems for safekeeping. Now weeds
are plowed down, the animals gone.

On the other side of the field there is still
the Eucalyptus grove that edges an old spring
once used to heal a person's aches. Moss
of the wildest green used to grow there, haven
for tadpoles we'd bring home until frogs,
then let them go again like this, my poem
to you that houses hope for their return.

California Poets In The Schools

The Fish
For Grades Three Through Eight

by Iris Jamahl Dunkle

Elizabeth Bishop is one of the most important American poets of the twentieth century. Her images are precise and true to life, and they reflect her own sharp wit and moral sense. Her poem "The Fish" gives students an incredible example of what it is to experience the natural world and to realize that it is of great beauty but it is not ours to enter. In this lesson, students explore Bishop's method of describing an animal in great detail.

1. Begin by briefly introducing Elizabeth Bishop. Bishop was born in Massachusetts but spent important early years of her childhood growing up in Nova Scotia, Canada, with her grandparents. She also lived for several years in Brazil as an adult. She crafted and polished her poems with great care and didn't publish that many of them during her lifetime. She also painted and wrote short stories. (For more, see her biography on Poets.org and the Poetry Foundation website.)

2. Read "The Fish" aloud. (The poem can be found on the Poets.org website.) Before reading, make sure you take a moment to remind students that it's okay to not know all of the words in a poem. For example, in this poem Bishop uses a lot of nautical terminology, such as gunnels.

3. Ask questions about the poem. How does Bishop describe the fish when it was caught? How do you think she knows what the inside of the fish looks like? How does she feel about the fish? Did the fish teach her about herself? Did she keep the fish or let it go? Why?

4. Pass out photographs of animals to the students. Ask students to look closely at their animal and imagine that they have somehow caught this animal and that it is right in front of them. Have them consider the following questions:
   - Describe what your animal looks like now that it is caught.
   - Imagine what the inside of your animal looks like.
   - How are you like your animal?
   - How are you not like your animal?
   - What about this animal fascinates you?
   - What can you learn from this animal?
   - Finally, in the end, do you let the animal go or keep it? Why?

5. Pass out the worksheet and read the sample poems.

6. Choose one of the animal photographs and write a class poem on the board at the front of the room.

7. Ask the students to write their own poem.

8. Leave time for at least some students to share.

Time and Materials: A copy of "The Fish" by Elizabeth Bishop in a format you can share with the kids: on the document reader, projector, handouts, or chart paper; pictures of animals from nature magazines, calendars, books—enough for each child to have one to look at.

Worksheet

Turtle Pride
by Sarah Olson, Sonoma County

I envisioned a green sea
turtle   today,
with rivers of rain and water running off
her back, pursued by an
invisible
enemy. She is as
round
and
small
as a hamster, with
eyes as deep as the ocean.
Sprinkled with barnacles, she
emerged
victorious
from the treacherous journey through the ocean.
All muscle from enduring wave after wave of
cold
and
salt,
flippers as hard as steel, bone frame as supple
and flexible as a gymnast's. I watch in awe as
she
struggles
to the top of the beach and surveys her
domain, the
endless
expanse of the
ocean …

Just Like a Phoenix!
by Sophia de la Cruz, Sonoma County

The bright red fur like fire burning out,
his teeth so sharp like a dagger
waiting to attack,
the high-pitched scream,
so loud it hurt,
the nose so wet …and his eyes,
so yellow and
ferocious like the sun.
Like me, so intent when I hear
something like an enemy trying to attack.
His long bushy fox tail
bigger than his body …
Amazing as he was,
I saw fury in his eyes.
So I unhooked the latch
and there he went, running, jumping,
probably very happy and relieved he is free …

The Eternal Mystery
by Alec Hemphill, Sonoma County

I caught a great big snake bird
to see what he was like—
his feathers so black like a chalkboard,
his beak so long and straight like the tail
of a comet, his big blue eyes
like a blue jay's feather …
So light, so clear,
small white spots like the stars in the big,
outstretched sky …
Surrounded in eternal blackness,
his heart, beating like a gong,
his soul, free as the air, he was now incarcerated by me. I knew
he was terrified, just like anyone else who
was trapped.
He stared at me,
big blue puppy eyes,
and I thought,
"What have I done?"
This amazing creature,
scared, worried, terrified.
And I let him go …
Seeing the black bird walking away,
he looked back at me
as if he were sorry to leave me.
I wondered why.
I never saw him again.

Prompts
I caught a _____ today.
    (insert the name of your animal here)
My animal is like … with its …. (similes/metaphors)
Inside *my animal*, there is (*organ, entrails*) like….
Like me, *my animal* …
Unlike me, *my animal* …
_____ fascinates me because…
_____ teaches me….

In the end, do you let your animal go, or keep it?

California Poets In The Schools

Entering a Picture: Poetry from Visual Art For Grades Three and Up

by Seretta Martin

Is it possible for a lesson to appeal to all ages, beginner through advanced? Yes, this one does! I've taught it in elementary schools and high schools, in museums and senior centers. It stimulates the imagination in magical ways. Each student selects a picture for some personal reason. That reason is yet to be discovered in the writing of the poem. This lesson teaches attention to image, detailed descriptions, the senses, vocabulary research, personification, and more. Sometimes it triggers memories or uncovers unexpected desires. The student's *imagination* is stretched when prompted to crawl into the picture and become someone or something in that world.

    Start this lesson by projecting a few successful model poems and pictures on a screen. Read them, commenting on how the poet used unusual words and put herself or himself into the picture. Call on students to read. The model poems and pictures create excitement. Distribute writing paper and the worksheet. Place a batch of pictures on each table. Give students five minutes to select a picture. Collect extra pictures so students are able to focus on the one picture that they have chosen for their poem.

1. Enter into the painting. Let your mind wander. Think about how you would describe it to a blind person. Your poem is going to paint a picture with words. Pay close attention to details. Remember, a blind person needs lots of information to visualize the picture. What do you see in the painting? colors? patterns? figures? What do you feel? Write what first comes to mind. Does the art remind you of a memory, a family member, a friend, or something you lost?

2. Describe the scene. Is it a meadow? an attic? a candy jar? your front porch? the edge of a volcano? Think about your five senses and write using rich details. Describe smells, sounds, tastes, colors, and what things feel like to touch. Are they rough or silky or what?

3. What is happening? Use action words. For example, perhaps the creature in your poem does some of these things: sings, growls, chomps, leaps, glides, races, dances, or slouches. Make your poem come to life with colorful *strange* words. Avoid "worn-out" words and use a thesaurus to find substitutions. Use strong images.

4. What is not in the picture? Imagine what happened before or after what you see. Crawl into the picture and become a person, animal, or object. Maybe you want to take the point of view that you are speaking with someone or some object. You may want to use some dialog.

5. Ask yourself questions: Is my first line or stanza so interesting that it will make the reader want to read my poem? Do I want to make my most exciting idea my first line? Have I used words that paint a clear picture? Do I want to repeat any words to make my poem more musical (lyrical) or to emphasize something?

6. How will you end your poem? a surprise? by revealing a secret? an unexpected twist? a question? Or will you end with a good line of dialog? What do you want the reader to feel? Think of a unique title that pulls the reader in, but don't give away too much too soon.

Time and Materials: One to 1 1/2 hours. Include time for students to read their poems and project pictures. You will need images from art galleries, fine arts prints, postcards, magazines, calendars, and so on, plus a thesaurus, a projector, and paper clips (to clip pictures to poems at the end of the class); and word lists of the five senses, emotions, worn-out words, action words. Optional adult poems: "The Starry Night" by Anne Sexton, "White Wedding Slippers" by Anna Swir, "Cezanne's Ports" by Allen Ginsberg, "Van Gogh's Bed" by Jane Flanders, and "Mourning Picture" by Adrienne Rich. Optional student poems: From the *Border Voices Poetry Project* anthologies at bordervoices.com: "Empty Chairs" by Jasell Smith (2010), "The World of Things" by Brent Stewart (2011), and "The Date" by Rylie Willard (2013).

Worksheet

Shelf City
by Nathaniel Pick

I see half-fish-half-humans
playing guitars in the street.

Birds sit atop a lollipop tree.
Figures perch on skyscrapers
and bright-colored lights dance
in the windows.

The scent of wood
hangs in the air. Tacos, chips,
horchata, and tortillas sizzle . . .

I hear church chimes.
Tourists dance on a tour bus
followed by a horse-drawn
truck with a cab full of chickens.

Yes, this city is wonderful.
But when I stop imagining,
all sounds stop, smells fade,

and all the clay figures
lie on the shelf
waiting to be brought to life again.

The Silver Eclipse
by David Melendez-Perdomo

Outside our world of color
the glimmering eclipse
shines toward earth, so bright
we cover our eyes with dark glasses.

Watching its glow
in the shimmering air
we can taste the cold light
as we let our minds go out

free, in a trance, while the silver
slowly fades.

With one last flash
the eclipse ends, and there we are
in a trance, with silver light
dripping from our lips.

The Woman Who Lives on Wall Street
(after a sidewalk drawing)
by Dylan Love

People walk over her every day.

She wears lots of clothing all at once
and has a barcode skirt.

The woman of Wall Street is frozen
in the same position.

She smells like the pleasant aroma of hot dogs
from the vendor cart down the endless street.

Her left leg is bright orange and her right leg
is still being drawn by the chalk artist.

The woman waits for the earth to quake
and pop her out of the sidewalk.

I am the two-dimensional woman
who lies on the sidewalk, aching to be
      three-dimensional.

Big Brown Eyes
by Sage Gautier

In the painting she sits barefoot on a step,
her dark hair matted, her lonely brown eyes
pleading for answers.

She has paused to rest, the fiddle
quiet in her lap, her hands callused
from fingering the strings. The bow
with three strings comforts her with music.

Her roots can be traced to back alley
and dirt roads in London.
She owns one gray dress two sizes too large
and a handmade shawl from a loved one
now in a place she's waiting to go.

In her blurry vision, an audience cheers
as they listen to the forlorn melody of her fiddle
and drop change on the pavement in front of her.
She sits and fantasizes
the life she is longing to experience.

All student poets are from San Diego County.

Word Pictures and Hieroglyphics: The Birth of Writing
For Grades Three Through Six

by Arthur Dawson (inspired by Terry Ehret and Maureen Hurley)

This lesson sparks imaginative thinking almost effortlessly. It works well with upper elementary grades, but has been successful with everyone from preschoolers to adults. It's very flexible and versatile—good for an introductory lesson or much later in a residency. Though it's based on visual metaphors, it can be "loaded up" with whatever else you like: the use of the senses, sound play, etc. Strip down the introduction and it serves as a fun free write. Or extend the intro with a class discussion about the invention of writing and imagining a world without the written word.

1. Ask: "How was the alphabet invented?" It started out as pictures. Draw an upside-down *A* on the board. Ask: "What does this look like besides an upside-down *A*?" People used this symbol to count their cattle, drawing it on clay tablets. It meant "one cow." At some point, they realized they could use this symbol to stand for a sound. You can still hear the sound of *A* in the word *ox*. (This is the 'a' sound in *calm, palm,* or *swallow*.) I wonder why the *ox* ended up on its back?
2. Not everyone substituted sounds for pictures. Chinese characters still stand for whole words. Here's an example showing how Chinese creates complex meanings from simple pictures:

Two legs = PERSON

Person with arms stretched out = BIG

The big thing over our heads = SKY, HEAVEN

3. Ancient Egyptians used hieroglyphs to represent whole words. Here's one of them:

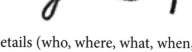

4. Class brainstorm: Ask what does this remind you of? Write their ideas on the board.
5. Class poem: Ask a student to choose one of the ideas. Students add details (who, where, what, when, how) to create a whole image (such as "a salmon resting in a calm green pool"). Repeat the process several times until you have a class poem.
6. Optional: Pass out the worksheet with sample poems and hieroglyphs. Choose a student to read each one out loud. Discuss where the ideas in the poem came from, and which ones echo back to the hieroglyph.
7. Pass out individual hieroglyph cards and explain the easiest approach (students can of course do something completely different or use hieroglyphs from the worksheet):
   - Look at your card, turning it different directions.
   - Write down one or two word ideas for what it looks like or reminds you of. Leave a couple of lines between each idea.
   - When you have several ideas written down, go back and add details to create full images, just as we did with the whole class.
   - Draw your hieroglyph next to your poem.
8. Optional: Pass out one or two *word* cards to each student that they can use if they want.

Time and Materials: One hour (including a review of the preceding lesson and a warm-up exercise of your choice). You will need index cards with hieroglyphs, Chinese characters, and Roman letters.

Worksheet

There are waterfalls
by Terry Ehret

There are waterfalls in the rainforest tangled up in this life. Her hair tumbles down her back in a long braid. It buys expensive rooms high above the city. Boats fall out of the horizon into the ocean, traveling long white wakes as they come back to the bay. She is made of two strands. Now she braids her long hair with flowers.

A lake. A night without a moon
by Terry Ehret

A lake. A night without a moon. Distant memory of what the sun looks like rising. The darkness blows across the water like a wind. Passions that cool with age.

W
by Laurel Moeslein, Sonoma County

W is two sides
fighting
a mother on one side
a daughter on the other.
Two people
who share the same blood
separated
by a wounding wall.
Two sides.
Two kin.
One wall.

Raindrop
Class poem, Sonoma County

A raindrop
glides in the air
like a star
falling from the sky;
it is a needle
sewing a ripped shirt up.

Prompts
Ask yourself: If my hieroglyph was part of an animal or person, what would it be? If it was a tool, what would it be used for? Add details by asking : Who? Where? When? What? How? Why? If your hieroglyph looks like a broken chair, ask yourself: How did it get broken? Who broke it? Why did they break it? Where is the chair?

California Poets In The Schools

Japanese Tanka: From the Concrete to the Ephemeral For Grades Three Through Eight

by Phyllis Meshulam

Kids need no special preparation for this lesson, but I especially like to teach tanka at the end of the school year when they are saying goodbye to a classroom or sometimes even graduating to a new school. I put no pressure on young people to conform to the exact syllable count. I like the other feature of these short poems – they tend to start with something concrete and move from the physical to the emotional. I ask the students: "What physical things will you remember about this time of your life? What emotions are these things charged with?"

1. Explain how Japanese children, by the time they reach sixth grade, have memorized one hundred tanka poems, chosen from ones written over many centuries. In Japan, they may be given cards with pictures illustrating the poem—along with one line of it—on one side. On the other is the complete poem. These cards are numbered from *one* to *one hundred*, arranged in chronological order from the oldest to the newest. On the worksheet, you'll see something that resembles a Japanese tanka card. These cards are also used to play a game that is as popular in Japan as *Monopoly* is in the United States!
2. Point out that the form consists of five lines. Traditionally, the syllable count is: first line—five syllables, second—seven, third—five, fourth—seven, fifth—seven. The first three lines are just like a haiku in terms of syllable count. Most lines are not sentences. This form doesn't have to be strictly followed in English, but it's good to vary short and long lines.
3. Read the traditional example on the worksheet, and notice how it moves from mountains to sadness. That's the other thing typical of these poems—they start with something concrete and physical, and then move into the mood and emotion. Can the students see/feel the progression?
4. Have the kids brainstorm a list of objects they connect with this classroom, or their whole career at this school—now that they are leaving it. Record a bunch of these on the board. Examples: soccer field, bench where you would get benched, cafeteria, traffic circle in front, band room, water fountain, uniforms, detention notices … (Discourage the generic "friends" as a topic. It's too hard to be specific with a group.)
5. Read examples of tanka by students of previous years. Notice that ALL the lines are pretty short, and most aren't sentences.
6. Try a group poem—on the subject of something that the class as a whole can relate to, guiding the kids to start with concrete details, and end with an expression of the feeling. For example:
    - "Let's pick one of the topics we brainstormed. What's something you can all relate to?" Someone says "water fountain," someone else, "boys' bathroom." "Well let's go with 'water fountain' so we can *all* relate to it. That could be our first line. *Water fountain*."
    - "Now, help the reader *see* that water fountain, the one you all know." Another hand goes up, another student suggests "silver." "Silver as what?" Another voice: *Silver as a nickel*.
    - "Can we use any other of our five senses to help us remember it?" *Cold water.* "Okay, we have three lines! Our next line could be a little longer if we want.
    - What is special about this water fountain that you want to remember?" "People jam it and you get sprayed." "Use details. What do they jam it with?" *People jam it with gum and you get sprayed.*
    - "Fabulous! Only one more line. Time to show some emotion. What feeling might you have about this whole thing?" *But without water there is no life.* (With thanks to the 6th graders in Room 10 at Monroe School, spring 2013.)
7. Give students quiet writing time to compose their own. Share.

Materials: A board, chart paper, or document reader where you can generate a list of concrete objects from the school.

Worksheet

by Sarumaru, ninth-century Japan

In the deep mountains,	(five)
cutting through the autumn leaves,	(seven)
the cry of the deer.	(five)
When I hear it,	(traditionally seven)
autumn sadness, loneliness.	(seven)

(Translated by Paula Doe)

by Angel Cruz, Sonoma County

Two-story building
with its long fleet of stairs.
Tiring.
Tallest building in the school.
Glad I won't have to climb the stairs any more.

by Rogelio Cruz, Sonoma County

Yellow monkey bars.	(short)
Swinging from metal bar to metal bar.	(long)
Blisters on our hands.	(short)
Racing each other to the other end.	(long)
Sorry, monkey bars, but we have to leave.	(long)

Advice to Writers
Pick one of the topics that we brainstormed, or think of one of your own. Just be sure it's concrete: something you can touch, see, smell, hear. Go from the physical thing to the emotional feeling that it gives you. Try a variety of long and short lines.

The Poem Is in Your Life (Memory) For Grades Four Through Six

by Gail Newman

I like to talk to students about how writers get ideas from their lives and experiences. I tell them about my own childhood and how those memories have stayed with me. Any ordinary day can be full of poetry. I find the student poems are richer if this lesson is presented after the children have studied metaphor and simile. It also works well when preceded by a lesson on writing in response to art.

1. Tell the students: "Here is a poem by Ellen Bass about a time she lost her dog. Ellen Bass lives in Santa Cruz, California, and has written four books of poetry. She says, 'Very often a poem comes from something I'm trying to work out in my own life.' " Read "Lost Dog."
2. Ask: "Have you ever lost anything?" Discuss.
3. Ask: "What happens in the first part of the poem?" Read the first stanza again. "What visual things do you notice?" (Children like to count and compare notes. This is a good time for "pair share.") "What happens next? How does the poet feel?"
4. "What other senses does the poet use to describe the scene?"
5. "Do you notice any similes or metaphors in the poem? How can a heart be like a racetrack?"
6. Write a collaborative poem on the board, using the model of the questions below. Say: "Picture a time and place you remember when you had a strong feeling: sad, scared, or excited."

QUESTIONS	SAMPLE ANSWERS
Where are you?	*In the garden.*
What are you doing?	*Drinking tea and eating lemon cookies.*
Who else is there?	*Eli and my grandma.*
What do you see, hear, smell?	*We hear the birds flying around.*
What are things doing?	*My chair is wobbling on the grass.*
What is the weather like?	*The fog is like a ghost covering the trees.*
How do you feel? (simile)	*I feel like I am hugging the world.*

7. "Here are some poems written by kids your age." Read the sample poems by Perry and Grady.
8. "Now you can write your own memory poem. You can picture a time and place—the same or a different one—when you had a strong feeling: sad, scared, or excited. It could be yesterday, this morning, or a long time ago. Pretend your mind is a camera, and take a picture. If you close your eyes while I talk, you may see the picture more clearly in your mind."
9. Ask the above questions again while the children close their eyes. (They may want to put their heads down on their desks.) Add more detail as you talk: "Are you inside or outside? In a house, library, hospital? Are you sitting, standing, lying down? What colors do you see? Look on the ground. Look up. If you hear voices, what are they saying?"
10. "When you are ready, open your eyes and begin writing. You can answer the questions or just write whatever comes into your mind."
11. Write. Share.

Materials: Optional: You can find a photograph of Ellen and her dog at othervoicespoetry.com. A copy of the questions in # 6—on the board, chart paper, or suitable for projecting.

Worksheet

Lost Dog
by Ellen Bass

It's just getting dark, fog drifting in,
damp grasses fragrant with anise and mint,
and though I call his name
until my voice cracks,
there's no faint tinkling
of tag against collar, no sleek
black silhouette with tall ears rushing
toward me through the wild radish.

As it turns out, he's trotted home,
tracing the route of his trusty urine.
Now he sprawls on the deep red rug, not dead,
not stolen by a car on West Cliff Drive.
Every time I look at him, the wide head
resting on outstretched paws,
joy does another lap around the racetrack
of my heart. Even in sleep
when I turn over to ease my bad hip
I'm suffused with contentment.

If I could lose him like this every day
I'd be the happiest woman alive.

Sickness
by Grady Benjamin Collins, San Francisco County

I am on my sofa getting
better on a Wednesday
at noon, a fog bank slowly
watching and walking by my window
with me and my sister. I can smell
the slowly walking
fog but I feel
the blanket like a woven
warmth. I see the dull gray like
fine sand smothered every
where but me.

Friends
by Perry F. H. Yun, San Francisco County

On a Saturday afternoon
I was skipping along
with my best friend Grace
to her house, the wind like
fierce tigers on our shoulders,
the fog withering like a fish
out of water.
When we got to her house
the fireplace was crackling merrily
like a happy witch
whose concoction had worked.
Then we leapt happily in each other's
arms in a round hot snowball.

친구들

시인: 윤희진

어느 토요일 오후
나의 절친 그레이스와 함께 달렸다.

바람은
호랑이 처럼
우리 어깨 위에 으르렁 거렸다.
안개는
물에서 나와있는 물고기 처럼
살아졌다.

집에 도착하니
벽난로는
주술에 선공한 마녀 처럼
명랑하게 낄낄 웃었다.
그리고 우리는
뜨거운 눈덩이 처럼
서로를 껴안고 잠이 들었다.

(Translated by Perry Yun into Korean)

Advice to Writers
Focus on the picture and the feeling. Do stay in one place for a while. The questions are just to help you see the details. Please write whatever comes into your mind.

Wild Mind (Chant: Slant and Internal Rhyme) For Grades Four Through Six

by Claudia Poquoc

Writing chant poems offers an integrated approach to learning. In Native American traditions, chants help develop constructive relationships to all things. They meet curriculum needs by letting the class experiment with language patterns and respond creatively to a multitude of stimuli. This lesson brings in the musicality of rhythm and repetition, as well as rhyme. It is a dynamic way to introduce performance poetry. And it works well with students who speak English as a second language.

1. (10 minutes) Begin by introducing the students to rhythm. If space allows, I always get students up and out of their seats to do this. You can have them copy a rhythm you perform using stomping, clapping and other gestures, or you can use a drum. Or I may put on a drumming CD that uses simple beats. I keep rhythm with it by tapping different parts of my body or stomping my feet, and the students copy me. I may even invite some of them to create their own gestures to the rhythms, and then we all copy them. They love doing this.

2. (15 minutes) When they're back in their seats, we make lists of possible topics: animals as persons (give examples: Yogi bear, Winnie the Pooh, Nemo); names of trees, flowers, and weeds; planets, moon, constellations and their movements; dreams; human love; the five senses and also the sixth intuitive sense; the ecstasy of the dance; what we find in darkness or when we close our eyes; and what we may find in silence. Make a list on the board or on a flip chart of key words or phrases you think the students might like to write about. (Or have a list available as a handout.)

3. (5 minutes) Students choose just one theme that they will write four to eight lines about. These can be phrases or sentences. Read examples from the worksheet, reminding them that, for now, they are only writing the "in between" lines, not the full chants.

4. (20 minutes) Using made up sounds found on the worksheet, or ones that they create, students write out a poem inserting those sounds between each English line. If necessary, plan to continue developing this at the next session. Plan to have students read their poems out loud as time permits. Vary it with the entire class reciting the made up sounds of a poem, for example.

Time and Materials: Plan for at least one fifty-minute session, although the lesson can be carried over into another one. It is helpful to have a drum, or rattle to use for variation, and/or a CD player and a CD with a simple rhythm. You will also need a white board, flip chart, or document reader for lists of topics and vocabulary, especially action verbs, plus writing paper, folders, or journals.

Worksheet

Turkey Talk
by Claudia Poquoc, poet-teacher

The earth she turns to find the light
   Ya-he Aho Wayo
She eats the light to grow new life
   Ya-ho Wayo Haya
The wild turkey struts around
   Ya-he Aho Wayo
He bobs his head and scrapes the ground
   Ya-ho Wayo Haya
From the meadow up he climbs
   Ya-he Aho Wayo
He leaves a feather for me to find
   Ya-ho Wayo Haya

Note: The adjacent poem uses internal and slant rhyme, with repetitive sounds between the lines. The lines in quotations are what the magpie sings in Gary Snyder's poem "Magpie's Song." Excerpts used with permission of Gary Snyder.

Advice to Writers
Write four to eight lines about nature or other experiences. Between each line, write these made up sounds or invent two lines of your own sounds:
        Ya-he Aho Wayo
        Ya-ho Wayo Haya.

Magpie's Song
adapted by Claudia Poquoc

Waya, Hayo
"Here in the mind, brother
Turquoise blue."
Waya, Hayo
Here in the heart, sister
Turquoise green.
Waya Hayo
"I wouldn't fool you.
Smell the breeze
It came through all the trees"
Waya Hayo
"No need to fear what's ahead
Snow up on the hills west
Will be there every year
be at rest."
Waya Hayo
"A feather on the ground—
The wind sound—"
Waya Hayo
"Here in the Mind, Brother,
Turquoise Blue"
Waya Hayo
Here in the heart, Sister,
Turquoise green.
Waya Hayo, Waya Hayo, Waya Hayo

California Poets In The Schools

Where Poems Hide (Personification, Anaphora, Narrative) For Grades Three and Up

by Tresha Faye Haefner

This lesson gives kids a chance to talk about unusual things they love, while also allowing them to fiddle around with figurative language. I recommend it for students who already know something about poetry and have a connection with it, or who are just starting to figure out what poetry is and need nudges to understand where to "find" a poem. This is also an opportunity to show students what an anaphora poem looks like.

1. Review the term *personification* and ask students for examples. You could mention that the ancient Greeks were very good at personification, especially at turning emotions into people. That's where the idea of Eros, or Cupid (a later Roman name), came from. The emotion of "love" was personified as a little boy with wings who shot arrows at you to make you fall in love. Poets often write of inanimate objects doing things that people do.
2. See Gail Newman's "Shy Sky" lesson (page 36) for a further explanation.
3. Once you feel the students understand personification, read Naomi Shihab Nye's poem "Valentine for Ernest Mann." Ask students if they can spot the personification in the poem. For example: "Do you think poems *really* sleep? Or play hide-and-go-seek?"
4. Note that Nye says that poems can "hide" anywhere, even on the bottom of your shoe, and that the man in the poem saw poems hiding in the eyes of a skunk.
5. Ask the students to write down at least ten things that they themselves find special and beautiful, interesting, and/or worth writing about that other people don't like or know about at all. You may want to draw the connection that poems "hide" in places that have special meaning for us.
6. Read Hana's and Monica's poems out loud together. Notice how Monica's tells a story, making a narrative poem.
7. Now have students look at their own lists and use at least five items from their list of things that are special to them to write a poem answering the question, "Where do poems hide?"
8. Tell students that if they are stuck, they may try writing the poem as an anaphora poem. Explain that this is a poem in which every line starts with the same word or phrase. They may try just repeating the phrase "Poems hide" and finishing the rest off with the different places they might find poems.
9. At the end of class, ask everyone to share their poems. Choose one line from each student in the room (preferably a line that completes the phrase "Poems hide") and write it down on the board as part of a class-wide anaphora poem. Or you can collect papers, extract these lines, and bring the group poem back for your next session.

Time and Materials: This lesson should take a full hour, especially if you are including the group-poem portion of the lesson. It can take less time if you let students work on their own and allow limited time for sharing. You will need a copy of Naomi Shihab Nye's poem, "Valentine for Ernest Mann," in the form of a hand-out or a copy to put in the document reader. It was published in 1994 in *Red Suitcase* and can be found online.

Worksheet

Where Poems Hide
by Hana Kraus, Los Angeles County

Poems hide like a diamond in the rough.
They hide in a place where one's too afraid to enter,
but when brought to life,
a beautiful ensemble of letters, words and phrases,
dappled in the golden rays of discovery can be found.
They hide in the shadows, evading the prying eye
of the flashlight beam.
They hide,
stuck in cobwebs,
in an old tortoise shell,
between violin strings,
under rocks lost in the tide,
beneath Hebrew characters,
behind the oppressive veil of Sharia law.
They hide in a Shinto shrine,
in a Buddhist monastery off the beaten path.
They hide in a frozen lake,
protected by a dark green, frigid veil.
Poems hide in the cracks of pavement.
They hide in the iridescence of a hummingbird,
in a child's first breath of life.
They hide in the farthest depths of the sea,
where everything is so dark you can see the stars
and how the universe itself was made,
poems are found so deep you have to waltz
around the Milky Way sometimes
to reach them with your fingertips
in the dregs of green tea.

Hello, My Name Is Poetry
by Monica Carris, Los Angeles County

It woke up one night
And forced me to listen to it
It knocked on my door
And told me its name was poetry
I asked it how old it was
It asked me right back "How old am I?"
I asked it where it came from
"How am I supposed to know?" it chuckled
I asked it where it lived
It responded, "Anywhere you can find me.
But if you have to chase me, I promise you will never catch me."
And then it left
Before I could open my mouth to ask it to explain itself
It was gone
It came
It confused me
Then it left
I tried to run after it
Then I remembered that it was no use
So I sat and I waited, hoping that it would come back to me
But sitting and waiting doesn't get you anywhere
So I went to bed
And when I woke up
It was there
It was everywhere
In the radiance of the early-morning sun
In the smell of the fresh dew on the grass
In the song of the blue jay high in the oak tree
Even in the oak tree itself
In fact, it was all over that ordinary oak tree
At least, it seemed ordinary yesterday
Has it always been there,
This thing that introduced itself as poetry?
It must have been
Of course it has
I was convinced of it
I just never thought I would spend the rest of my life
Convincing everyone else of it, too.

Advice to Writers

You can write your poem like a list, just like Hana did in the first sample poem, above. Or, you can write your poem like a short story where you meet poetry and it says or does something. Both are great ways to answer the question, "Where do poems hide?"

My Heart
For Grades Three Through Twelve

by Dan Zev Levinson

Our hearts are powerful muscles, receiving and driving our lifeblood throughout our bodies. They are so important that ancient cultures believed they held the mind and soul. We still touch our chests to indicate strong feeling or respect or connection, and we say that our hearts hurt, are broken, are overflowing with love or joy or grief. The heart commands the pulse of life and represents our deepest core. It also provides our earliest sense of rhythm. The first poems are said to have been composed to the rhythm of the heartbeat, as well as to the rhythm of walking. The heart is the ideal metaphor on which to base a poem about ourselves, what's inside of us, what we express, or are afraid to let out.

1. Say: "We're going to write poems about our hearts today. What do you think I mean by that?" Encourage discussion of literal and metaphorical meanings of "heart." Continue: "The heart, with its rhythm and emotion, is the ideal metaphor on which to base a poem about ourselves, what's inside of us, what we express, or are afraid to let out."

2. Read sample poems on worksheet. Ask: "What did you like? What metaphors did you see?"

3. Say: "Think about your life for a moment, about the long journey that brought you to this point. Are you happy or sad, or both? At peace with the world? Angry? Let's start by writing down one metaphor or simile that describes or embodies your heart. In other words, fill in this blank: My heart is (like)_____." Give the students a little time to write down one example on their papers. Then ask for volunteers to share, reminding the class that they're getting into a world of things that can be private and sensitive—so as listeners we'll share only positive reactions. As the teacher you can set a tone of gentle admiration.

4. Present the questionnaire on the worksheet. Say: "Let's start by trying a group poem. Our hearts are all different, though they may be surprisingly similar in some ways. Maybe we'll discover what the heart of the class is like." Go through the questionnaire getting individuals to contribute lines from different questions. Write these on the board, or get a student to jot them onto a piece of paper. You can guide their ideas. "What might the heart be made of? You can choose from building materials, art supplies, fabrics, animals, foods, things in nature."

5. Advise writers to go beyond fill-in-the-blank. Say: "Add details. Notice how Maisie doesn't just say, 'My heart is made out of memories.' She says, 'My heart is made out of old memories that sometimes shout out.'"

6. "Let's work quietly so everyone can hear what their own heart has to say."

7. When it's time to share, remind students to be especially respectful with this topic.

Materials: Worksheet. Writing materials.

Worksheet

My Heart
by Devon Garlick, Humboldt County

a heart is something that
can love but would really
rather not my heart
squeals and snorts pulls and tramples
to get away from love my
heart is an angry horse
a wild thing

Small Heart
by Maisie Moore, Humboldt County

My heart is a lonely
 child on a swing. Deep
  within my heart is love that
   has never been borrowed.
    My heart carries flexible
     metal. My heart is made
      out of old memories
       that sometimes shout
        out. My heart is
         thirsty for
          sepia-toned lovers that
           once laughed but
            now all that is
             left is old record
              players and photos.
               My heart sounds
                like a skipping
                 CD not able
                  to move
                   forward or move
                    back. My heart
                     misses what
                      it once had,
                       love to
                give out, love in return.

Love Struck
by Zev Levinson, poet-teacher

My heart is a sunburnt tomato.
Young its sweet seedy juice
moved mouths exploring Mediterranean salad,
perfected *la baguette nue avec du fromage*.

My heart is a departing dragonfly.
Iridescent wings once dazzled whole picnics,
swarmed meadows, lit upon a summer
creek's stone, the sparkliest crown jewel.

My heart is a deformed bowling ball.
How the pins danced with my spin,
its obsidian sheen mesmerizing eyes,
planets plucked from their orbits.

My heart is a mixed metaphor,
carbuncular fruit stealing heat from the sun,
darting insect ostensibly mythical,
wobbling down a lonely, broken lane,

leaking seared sugar,
stubbornly pounding its torn, translucent wings,
gambling on a lucky strike,
just trying to feel the beat.

Prompts

My heart is _____
In(side) my heart is/are _____
My heart holds/carries _____
My heart is made of _____
My heart is hungry/thirsty for _____
My heart sounds like _____

Put your own spin on the poem. Make it yours, different
from all the others. What else is happening with your heart?

California Poets In The Schools

Pantoums (Repetition)
For Grades Three Through Twelve

by John Oliver Simon, Artistic Director Poetry Inside Out,
Former Statewide Coordinator CPitS

The pantoum, a poetry form invented in Malaysia and brought west by the French poet Victor Hugo, will enable students to achieve astounding feats of repetition while letting their minds soar free wherever they will wander. If they learn this simple pattern, they will never be at a loss for how to begin or end a poem!

1. Share Lily Stoner's poem, bilingually if possible (a student may read Spanish if the instructor doesn't).
2. If time permits, tell a mature class about Delmira Agustini, whom Lily quotes for her line A. The first great woman poet of Uruguay, she lived a scandalous life, wrote very explicit love poetry, and was shot and killed by her husband because she wanted a divorce.
3. Ask for observations about the repetition. How many stanzas in the poem? How many lines in each stanza? How many total lines in the poem? If each line is repeated once, how many different lines in the poem?
4. If time permits, work through the pattern on the board, labeling lines 1 and 16 A, lines 2 and 5 B, etc. Students will help fill in the pattern. Hand out a worksheet with the pantoum form.
5. Ask what is the most important line in the poem (A, because it begins and ends the poem). It's also possible to do as Lily did and choose great first lines from beloved poems.
6. If time permits, compose a class pantoum on the board, accepting contributions from students.
7. Ask students to come up with their A line and write it in as both line 1 and line 16, checking with the instructor before going on.
8. Encourage students to write lines that are semi-independent units, as in Lily's poem, rather than a run-on narrative that will get fatally tangled by the pattern.
9. Students should compose a line, then fill it into its other slot as they go along. That way they know what's coming up. Some upcoming lines will be "sandwiched" between two already created lines and must fit somehow.
10. A pantoum can be created quickly. Soon students are writing the G and H lines, which complete (but do not end) the pantoum.
11. Read aloud.
12. Return to the pantoums in another session and revise them for clarity and originality.

    Pantoum Form

    A _____   E _____
    B _____   G _____
    C _____   F _____
    D _____   H _____

    B _____   G _____
    E _____   C _____
    D _____   H _____
    F _____   A _____

Time and Materials: One or two fifty-minute sessions (if two sessions are available, work on Lily's poem and get as far as a class pantoum the first day, then write original pantoums the second day). A third session for revision is optional. A larger version of the pantoum form above, reproduced as a worksheet. Have available some vivid first lines from other poets, famous or not.

Worksheet

"Gota de nieve con sabor de estrellas"
— *Delmira Agustini, 1886–1914*
 by Lily Stoner, Alameda County

Gota de nieve con sabor de estrellas
Pétalos de flor con crema de fresa
Nubes con canela de amor y leche
Paz con una tacita de cariño

Pétalos de flor con crema de fresa
Helado de hadas con chocolate
Paz con una tacita de cariño
Galletas de ángeles con irises

Helado de hadas con chocolate
Luna con lágrimas tan brillantes
Galletas de ángeles con irises
Olas bajando y subiendo, siempre

Luna con lágrimas tan brillantes
Nubes con canela de amor y leche
Olas bajando y subiendo, siempre.
Gota de nieve con sabor de estrellas.

"Drops of snow tasting of stars"
 by Lily Stoner, Alameda County

Drops of snow tasting of stars
Flower petals with strawberry cream
Clouds with cinnamon of love & milk
Peace with a little cup of kindness

Flower petals with strawberry cream
Fairy-tale ice cream with chocolate
Peace with a little cup of kindness
Angel cookies with irises

Fairy-tale ice cream with chocolate
Moon with tears so shiny
Angel cookies with irises
Waves rising and falling forever

Moon with tears so shiny
Clouds with cinnamon of love & milk
Waves rising and falling forever
Drops of snow tasting of stars

As I Dream
 by Mehrnush Golriz, Alameda County

I can't think of anything,
music is flowing through my head
like intertwining grapevines
jumbled together in a knot.

Music is flowing through my head
like an avalanche of wonders
jumbled together in a knot
that's too complicated to explain.

Like an avalanche of wonders
covering my soul
that's too complicated to explain
as I dream.

Covering my soul
like intertwining grapevines,
as I dream
I can't think of anything.

Advice to Writers
Working in a fixed form can free your wildest inventions. In the pantoum, you only have to make up eight lines to get a sixteen-line poem with a hypnotic, compelling rhythm of repetition.

Mind of Tumbling Water (Line Breaks) For Grades Four Through Seven

by Phyllis Meshulam

Kids like water, and even an imaginary trip to a body of water is refreshing and intriguing to them. (Of course, if you can coordinate this with a classroom's *real* water explorations, all the better.) What's more, the river theme and the sample poems offer a concrete illustration of line breaks. I would use this lesson no earlier than mid-residency, after ones on metaphor and five senses.

1. Tell the class: "Today we are going to take an imaginary field trip to a river or other place of water."
2. Tell a little about Gary Snyder, the treasured nature and environmental poet of California, who has been influenced by Chinese and Japanese writing and art. Currently, a right twinkly old elf! His poem is found in its entirety in *Mountains and Rivers Without End*. But you may choose to just read the excerpt included here, about half the poem. Snyder told me that the Raven's Beak is also known as the Tatshenshini River, which starts in Canada and flows into the ocean in southeast Alaska. You may or may not want to share with your students that *tatshenshini* in the local language means "shitty beak!" Read the poem.
3. Ask: "What are some of your favorite parts of this poem?" Accept and appreciate all answers! "Does the poet write normal sentences? Are they even sentences? How many periods do you see?"
4. Brainstorm bodies of water. The idea is to list enough that *everyone* will see one they know, including a puddle.
5. Say: "Pick one of these. Have paper and pencil ready for when we get back. Close your eyes and listen to my voice—we'll take a quick trip in our imaginations. How do you get to your place of water? For a river, usually you have to climb down to it, somehow. What are you walking or scrambling on? Twigs, rocks, dirt, pine needles, sand, sidewalk? Damp or dry?"
6. "What's the temperature like? Hot or foggy-cool? What are the sounds like? Can you *hear* the water? Can you hear kids splashing and shouting? Imagine putting your hand in. Is it icy or just cool? What's on the bottom? What plants or animals do you see?"
7. "What is one thing that stands out to you? Come back to this room and write down the word of the most special thing you saw. It's important, but your poem will be about more."
8. Share a few of the special words and then share Katie's poem. "What parts do you like?"
9. "These poets are using what I call the 'give me a break, give me a line break' poetry tool—an important one. You can emphasize certain words and change the pace of your poem. Play with this as you write today. You may want to make your special word stand out."
10. "Let's make a group poem. See the phrases at the bottom of your worksheet? Where it says 'signposts?' Use some phrases like those to take someone to *your* body of water. Who wants to start? Okay, great! All one line, or do you want to 'give me a break, give me a line break?'"
11. "What next? All one line? Does someone want to use their special object in here somewhere? Shall we put it on a line by itself?" Create the poem together.
12. "Now you're all going to get a chance to write. You can enter your poem much as you find your way to your place: 'I find my way . . .' 'Following . . .' How many are ready to write?"
13. "If your poem is ready to flow right along, go for it. If you need help, raise your hand."
14. If anyone's stuck, tell them they can write about bathtubs, sinks full of dishes and soapy water, etc.
15. Write! Allow time for sharing.

Time and Materials: About an hour. You will need vocabulary posters of landscape words, colors, aquatic animals, weather, flowers, trees, rocks, water birds. Optional: Nature guides and bird, butterfly, and tree posters.

Worksheet

Raven's Beak River
At the End (*excerpt*)
  by Gary Snyder

Looking north
   up the dancing river
Where it turns into a glacier
   under stairsteps of ice falls
Green streaks of alder
   climb the mountain knuckles
Interlaced with snowfields
   foamy water falling
Salmon weaving river
   bear flower   blue sky singer
As the raven leaves her boulder
   flying over flowers
Raven-sitting high spot
   eyes on the snowpeaks,
Nose of morning
   raindrops in the sunshine
Skin of sunlight
   skin of chilly gravel
Mind in the mountains, mind of tumbling water,
   mind running rivers . . .
At the end of the ice age
  we are the bears, we are the ravens,
We are the salmon
   in the gravel
At the end of an ice age
Growing on the gravels
   at the end of a glacier
Flying off alone
   flying off alone
   flying off alone

Off alone

Puddle
  by Katie Breninger, Sonoma County

Hearing the sound of children playing
I look north,
then walk,
head down.
I stop.
Suddenly silence surrounds me.
At my feet, puddle.
See my reflection.
Crystal water still.
I smell sweet and salty air.
Tickles my nose.
It tastes as if it were once snow
from the winter's fine crystals,
ice at the top.
Puddle,
feels like a part of me.
Dog comes. Stops,
laps up all water.
Standing still,
I now have a missing part.

Prompts

What are the signposts along the way to your body of water? Try one of these:

"I find my way . . ." "We enter . . ."
"Looking north . . ."   "Leaving . . ."
"Following footprints . . ."
"I'll show you the way . . ."

Make short lines to move us along.
What is the sound, the touch, the smell, the taste of this place of water?
What sights do you see?

Writing Like Sappho (Sapphic Modernism) For Grades Four Through Twelve

by Iris Jamahl Dunkle

This is a poetry lesson about the ancient Greek poet Sappho, who lived in the sixth century B.C. The lesson aims to teach young poets how to write like Sappho, who is famous for revising past poetic images and ideas in order to create a new poetry that allowed for the female voice.

1. Begin by introducing the poet Sappho: "How many of you like mysteries, or like things that come from unlikely sources? The poet Sappho is a bit of a mystery herself. She lived around 2,700 years ago on the isle of Lesbos in ancient Greece and was greatly admired during and after her lifetime (Plato hailed her as 'the tenth Muse'). Little is known about the facts of Sappho's life, yet many have speculated a history and perhaps even invented a mythology about her based loosely on what few 'facts' are found in her poetry. Believe it or not, Sappho was once one of the first rap stars. She sang her poems accompanied by a lyre at huge dinner parties. Does everyone know what a lyre is?" (Show picture on the worksheet.) "The word *lyre* is where the word *lyric* comes from. What remains are only tiny fragments of her work, and some of these were found in the most unlikely places, like garbage dumps!"
2. Pretend you are pulling a crumpled, dirty piece of paper out of the wastebasket in the room. "Oh my gosh! Look what I just found in the wastebasket! It's a fragment of a poem!"
3. Read the fragment to the class. Talk about how strange it is that Sappho's poems were found in garbage heaps.
4. "Fragment 96" is a translation taken from two sources and blended together by me. Read it to the students from the crumpled piece of paper or the worksheet and talk about its meaning. Talk about what Sappho could mean by the phrase "rosy-fingered moon." Sappho not only echoes a powerful Homeric phrase, "rosy-fingered dawn," but she transforms it for her own poetic purpose. She chooses to refer to a feminine symbol of the moon as a way of expressing a woman's longing.
5. Discuss the idea "Make it new." Ask the students if they have ever heard part of a song remixed into another. What Sappho does is the same as remixing. If time permits, with older kids, read one of Hilda Doolittle's Sapphic Expansion poems (which are examples of H.D. reinventing Sappho) or Amy Lowell's opening passage of "The Sisters" (where she also reinvents Sappho).
6. Introduce the lesson: "Today we are going to write like Sappho!" Pass the worksheet with Sappho's fragments. Ask the students to take out a pen and underline or circle any words or phrases they like as you read some of Sappho's other fragments aloud. Ask students to use these words or phrases as a jumping-off point: "Take a word, a phrase, or even an idea and (like H.D.) free associate about it. Feel free to bring in references to anything: your daily life, ancient Greece, a TV show you're reminded of—it doesn't matter where you pull your associations from. What matters is what these free associations mean to you. Use them as a means to tell your own story." Read some of the sample poems.
7. Write a class poem. Ask students if any phrase really draws them in (if they can't find one, use "rosy-fingered moon"). Ask the class to free-associate ideas or images that come to their minds when they hear this phrase. If they get stuck, find a new phrase and keep moving.
8. Let students begin writing.
9. Share.

Materials: A crumpled piece of paper with a fragment of a Sappho poem on it. For older students, you may want a copy of Amy Lowell's poem "The Sisters" (lines 13–34) to share with the class, or some of H.D.'s poems written to expand Sappho's fragments, including "Fragment Thirty-six," "Fragment Forty," "Fragment Forty-one," "Fragment Sixty-eight," and "Fragment 113," which can be found in H.D.'s *Hymen* (1921) and *Heliodora and Other Poems* (1924) or in her *Collected Poems, 1912-1944*.

Worksheet

Fragment 36

I know not what to do; my mind is divided.

Fragment 40

Now Love masters my limbs and shakes me,
fatal creature, bitter-sweet.

Fragment 93

As the sweet-apple blushes on the end of the bough,
the very end of the bough, which gatherers overlooked,
nay overlooked not but could not reach.

Fragment 94

As on the hills the shepherds trample the hyacinth underfoot,
and the purple flower [is pressed] to earth.

Fragment 113

Neither honey nor bee for me.

(Translations above by Henry Thornton Wharton)

After Sappho's Fragment 96
  by Iris Dunkle

. . . at Sardis . . . many times turning her mind in this
direction, [she thought] you were like a goddess,
and took joy in your singing. And now she stands out
among Lydian women, as, when the sun sets, the rosy-
fingered moon surpasses all the stars. She throws her light
across the salt sea and over flowering fields.

Camouflage
  by Madeline Miller, Sonoma County

I do not know what to do,
my mind is divided, distracted.
I am lingering, not yet wanting
to show my true identity: invisible.
Appearing black against a blue sky
a dark, purple, brown anger filled with misunderstanding
as I sink down, down, down
into the darkest night. I disappear.

The Liquid Moon
  by Zach Koehn, Sonoma Country

As I set foot upon the liquid moon
surpassing all stars, I bloom in the light
that encases me in gold. As I'm pulled to and fro,
flowers underfoot, the colorless, gloomy sky
consumes me in soot. Unknowingly, I'm released
from its cold grasp as the blooming sun
banishes the sky at last.

Dawn
  by Eduardo Lopez, Sonoma County

A moment ago gold-sandaled
dawn woke me up with
the voice of my mom.
She tells me to wake up
or the bus will leave me.
I get dressed and I put
on my golden-winged
sandals. I brush
my teeth and then
I grab my backpack
and go flying to
the bus stop.

Loneliness
  by Ethan Price, Sonoma County

I know not what to do. Light spreads alike
over the salt sea and the flowery fields.
A liquid moon glazed with rain water.
I know not what to do.
A wise tree sleeping beside a white cloud,
long branches dig deep in my soul.

A Cold Winter's Night
  by Ella Silvestrich, Sonoma County

My mind is much divided
like an apple cut in half
connected only through thinking
like two wings, but no bat.

California Poets In The Schools

Who's Your Muse?
For Grades Four Through Twelve

by Dan Zev Levinson

What inspires you? What are you passionate about? Can you embody these things in an almost-human, or perhaps superhuman, form? Most widely recognized are nine muses from Greek mythology, goddesses or spirits who inspire the creation of literature and the arts. Originally related in its root to *mind, mental,* and *memory,* the word *muse* persists in our language: *music, musing, amuse,* and *museum* (once a place where the muses were worshipped). We can stretch the notion beyond the arts, from sports to eating or cooking, from working with tools or machinery to simply relaxing. Who's *your* muse?

1. Write *music, amuse, museum, musing* on the board. What do these words have in common? Note the root, "muse."

2. Explain: "The ancient Greeks were really good at personifying things, especially emotions—giving them human qualities, and even thinking of them as gods. One thing that got personified was the idea of inspiration. When you get a really, really good idea, it's like some fairy or angel or shadowy person whispered it into your ear. The Greeks believed there were nine muses who could inspire you in history, poetry, dance, tragedy, comedy, astronomy, and music, etc."

3. In discussion, get the kids to name:
   - A favorite activity or a passion.
   - Something you want to improve at/in.
   - Something you want to do with your life, accomplish.
   - What inspires you? What are you passionate about?
   - Something that relaxes you.
   - Something that makes you happy.

4. Read some of the sample poems from the worksheet and get reactions.

5. Create a group list of possibilities on the board, including potential names of muses. Students can also list their anti-muses: what upsets, angers, distracts them, what keeps them from doing work: *Leafbloweria, Fluorescentia, Clocktickia, Dogbarkia* . . . This will create a group poem of the class's muses.

6. Don't scare away your muse while writing by worrying too much about spelling or by chatting with your neighbor. Your muse may be there whispering a good idea into your ear, and you need to pay attention to her or him while writing your draft.

7. Share.

Materials: White board; writing materials.

Worksheet

The Greek Muses

Name	Domain	Emblem
Calliope	Epic poetry	Writing tablet
Clio	History	Scrolls
Erato	Lyric poetry	Cithara (ancient musical instrument in the lyre family)
Euterpe	Music	Aulos (an ancient Greek musical instrument)
Melpomene	Tragedy	Tragic mask
Polyhymnia	Choral poetry	Veil
Terpsichore	Dance	Lyre
Thalia	Comedy	Comic mask
Urania	Astronomy	Globe and compass

O for a Muse of fire . . .
—*William Shakespeare, Henry V*

Sing for me, Muse, the mania of Achilles . . .
—*Homer, tr. Robert Lowell*

Sing in me, Muse, and through me tell the story . . .
—*Homer, tr. Robert Fitzgerald*

Susan's Muses
  by Susan Herron Sibbet, poet-teacher

Alarmina	The muse of waking early
Caffeina	The muse of making strong coffee
Persistina	The muse of sitting in the chair
Patienza	The muse of empty waiting
Silencia	The muse of quiet hope
Pushapena	The muse of putting the pen to paper
Focusina	The blind and deaf muse of writing no matter what
Finishina	The muse of knowing when to end

Alida's Own Traditional Muses of Life
  by Alida Nicklas, Humboldt County

1. *Amazonia*—
Is to help conserve our rainforests.
2. *Outsiden*—
A way of thinking outside the box.
3. *Thalia*—
Comedy can either make you feel better about yourself or worse. I choose better.
4. *Inspirationania*—
The people and themes that inspire me.
5. *Literaturania*—
Nothing impacts me more than a great book.
6. *Worldenlina*—
The power to change the world and make it better.
7. *Tutoris*—
I want to help peers improve in schoolwork or other things the best I can.
8. *Criticismalia*—
To be able to take criticism and make something of it.
9. *Emily Dickinsonina*—
Something/someone that inspires you.
10. *Originalina*—
To change tradition and start your own new one to follow.

My Muses
  by Andika Verick, Humboldt County

Bookonenia = muse of books
Aguania = muse of water
Aircaptinia = muse of pilots
Atmosferia = muse of the air
Entertania = muse of entertainment
Cyclania = muse of cyclists
Kayainia = muse of kayaking
Travilia = muse of travel
Oceana = muse of the ocean

California Poets In The Schools

Music Magic (Onomatopoeia, Lyricism) For Grades Five Through Twelve

by Phyllis H. Meshulam

Melopoeia ("music magic" to kids) is one of the three "magnetisms" of poetry, according to Ezra Pound. When words vibrate with musical qualities, they go beyond ordinary meaning. This lesson will help you use music as inspiration for your students. It's not a first lesson; use it after you've established some trust with the class and some enthusiasm for poetry. I also like to use "the drum" by nikki giovanni to teach this lesson. It's a tiny, powerful poem from *Spin a Soft Black Song*, and is available online.

1. Hang up your word posters and have your music ready before you start.
2. For kids who haven't been exposed to onomatopoeia, you can introduce them, using this fun approach from CPitS poet-teachers Daryl Chinn and Dan Levinson: Start a list on the board with words like *crash, snap, buzz*. Ask kids to volunteer to add to it, but not to identify what it's about yet. Other kids will catch on along the way. Eventually, get someone to articulate that these are words that sound like what they mean.
3. Discuss the sisterhood of poetry and music. "*Sonnet* means 'little song.' What else? Rap is right on the border between the two arts. In ancient Greece, poets didn't say their poems; they sang them accompanied by a stringed instrument called a lyre. You can use music to inspire your poems."
4. After this, share giovanni's short, defiant poem: a metaphor for the world as a drum and for wanting to make your own music with it. Say, "You'll have a chance to write what instrument you think the world is. And how you want to play it."
5. Before reading the excerpt of Robert Hass's poem to the class, tell a little about him: He was the poet laureate, or honored poet, of the United States for two years. He helped to create the River of Words international poetry contest for kids, and the Watershed Poetry Festival to raise environmental awareness. Explain that his poem is named for a biological study center in the Ecuadorian rainforest. Ask students to listen for the sounds and the music.
6. Ask students to tell you their favorite parts and/or to pick out words that remind them of a bell or other musical sounds.
7. Invite the class to read the student poem. Again, "What parts do you like?"
8. Say, "I'm going to put on some music now. As you listen, think of a metaphor for the world-according-to-you. It could be a musical instrument, a landscape, or any way you see the world. You don't need to write yet. We'll try a group poem first."
9. Stop the music after a few minutes and ask for some volunteers to share what they thought of. "Can anyone finish this phrase as a line of poetry? 'My world is a . . . that . . .'" Create a group poem, adding to this beginning. "What weathers do you blow? What colors do you strum or drum? What landscape contours do you trace on your keyboard, with your high notes or low notes? What happens to others when they listen to you?"
10. Allow the students to write their own poems. Turn the music up louder and encourage them to let it breathe into their words, inviting them to improvise, to surprise, and to be surprised.

Materials: You will need evocative instrumental music (and a means to play it), such as *Kind of Blue* by Miles Davis, especially cuts 3, 5, or 6; a copy of giovanni's poem, "the drum"; word posters about weather, colors, musical instruments, onomatopoeia, landscapes, kinesthetic verbs.

Worksheet

Jatun Sacha
(excerpt)
  by Robert Hass

First she was singing. Then it was a gold thing, her singing.
And her bending. She was singing and a gold thing.
A selving. It was a ringing before there was a bell.

Before there was a bell there was a bell. Notwithstanding.
Standing or sitting, sometimes at night or in the day,
when they worked, they hummed. And made their voices high
and made sounds. It was the ringing they hadn't heard yet
singing, though they had heard it, ringing.

When Casamiro's daughter went to the river and picked arum
    leaves,
and wet them, and rubbed them together,
they made the one sweet note that was the ringing.
It was the one-note cry of a bee-eating bird
with a pale blue crest, and when the first one
made the ringing with the arum leaves, and the others
heard that the arum leaves were the bee-eating bird,
they laughed. Their laughter rang. . . .

She sang like that, something of keening and something of laughing,
birth cries, and a gold thing, ringing.

The World of Me!
  by Erica Larson, Sonoma County

My world is a lonely trombone.
I will play rhythm and blues.
You can hear me through the lonely streets of Bluesville.
Listen: through all the twists, turns, giggles,
flip-flop, tingles, screaming and sound of cats
is a lonely trombone waiting to be noticed.
Notice me, it calls (slowly fading)
Notice me, it calls (slowly fading)

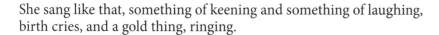

Advice to Writers

Listen and dream to the music. See how your pencil wants to move as you listen, what it wants to say. Remember the sound-rich words we talked about. Help yourselves to those, and to weather words, and color words, and landscape words. Need a sentence starter? Try one of these:

My world is a (musical instrument) that . . .

I will play (beat, strum, blow, hum) . . .

The music will sing (ring) like (about) . . .

The Heart's Book of Records (Superlatives) For Grades Four Through Seven

by Prartho Sereno

I often tell young poets that the best poem they can write is the one no one else can. This lesson evokes that kind of uniquely personal exploration. The idea came to me when I realized how popular the *Guinness Book of World Records* was with the gang of restless boys that had gathered at the back of the room. By starting with this book, restless boys are often first to get involved, eager to talk about the longest fingernails and the most piercings. It's easy then to build on the excitement of the Guinness superlatives and do a quick 180, diving right into the subject realm.

1. Begin by asking which students know *The Guinness Book of Records.* (In all the schools I have taught, more than half the hands go up.) Allow students who are familiar with the book to describe what can be found there. Tell them to be specific; not just the longest, but the longest what? These details are compelling for most students, getting everyone involved. Meanwhile, keep a running list of the superlative words on the board: *fattest, smallest, most* _____, etc.
2. Notice how the list is composed of words either ending in *est* or preceded by *most*, and talk about superlatives—how they describe the furthest reaches of experience. Then talk about how Guinness finds its entries (measurement of various kinds).
3. Now for the 180. Talk about how these records define the world we have in common. (Legend has it that the book was commissioned to settle bar disputes!) But there is also the utterly subjective world of the human heart, and it has accumulated its own records, which no one can dispute.
4. This is a great opportunity to demonstrate the weakness of clichés. Ask the students to say the first thing that comes to mind: *What's the bluest thing?* Nearly everyone will say the sky or the sea. But there's a good chance the sky won't even be blue at the moment, and there are plenty of days the sea is green or gray. So clichés are not only overused and dead—they're often untrue.
5. Point out: "But if you ask yourself what the bluest thing *you* ever saw was, things get different. It may be the sea, but which one? The aquamarine of the Caribbean? Okay, but focus even more: When? Just before sunset? Or it might be something simply personal to you: My father's eyes when my sister came home from the hospital, or my puppy's eyes when I first held him."
6. Try some other superlatives during the class discussion. The *most beautiful* is a great one. Encourage moments that others might not find beautiful, but a particular student does. Get him/her to convince us of that beauty—with details.
7. Time to write. Two possibilities: either choose one quality and mine it in many different directions (in nature, among people, household objects, etc.), or circle six to eight superlatives (and yes, students can add their own) and make a list poem of heart's records.
8. As always, save time to read aloud.

Time and Materials: The discussion affords so much good teaching, you should plan to give it 20 minutes or more, then 20 for writing, and at least 10 to 20 minutes for reading aloud, for a total of one hour. You will need a white board and the worksheet.

Worksheet

The Heart's Book of World Records
a group poem from Marin County

The kindest thing is an old dog.
The kindest thing is a tuna sandwich cut into four triangles.
The wrinkliest thing is a very old elephant baking in the sun.
A tulip, a shell, a petal, the metal, they fall to the reddest man.
The most peaceful thing is someone's breath, barely sounding,
    but just enough to hear.
The longest thing is the hallway from your room to the outside world.
The bravest thing is the person who dares to soar, the one who dives—
a masterpiece of uncertainty, that is the bravest thing.
The hardest thing is to find your way through San Francisco.

Advice to Writers
Here are some possible topics:

Roundest	Smallest	Most Beautiful	Smoothest	Kindest
Greenest	Reddest	Most Peaceful	Noisiest	Slowest
Friendliest	Weirdest	Deepest	Longest	Highest
Wrinkliest	Easiest	Happiest	Most Difficult	Brightest
Quietest	Strangest	Sweetest	Wisest	Truest

Add some details:
1. . . . with its_____ (The reddest thing is an August fire with its ruby flames)
2. Senses: Add another sentence saying what it looks like. Sounds like? Tastes like? Smells like? Feels like?
3. Other details: Where? When? Weather, time of year, color, light.

Remember, poets: No one can argue with the records of your heart. You are the king or queen of that land. Just listen closely to your own memories and the images you have gathered and write them true.

I Am (Metaphor, Chant) for Kindergarten Through Grade Six

by Grace Grafton

with Variations for Grades Seven Through Twelve

by Susan Kennedy (adapted by Phyllis Meshulam)

Susan Kennedy and Grace Grafton are two veteran poet-teachers who offer variations on a favorite theme: the "I Am" poem. I enjoy combining these two lessons into one, starting with Kennedy's name-based introduction, then moving into Grafton's approach. But you can do either. Grafton's lesson uses "The Delight Song of Tsoai-talee" by N. Scott Momaday, and Kennedy's uses "The Song of Amergin." The former is easy to find online and the latter is included. In either lesson, the poetic technique to be developed is metaphor, while rhythm is reinforced.

1. G. G. I like to start by asking a couple of pre-poem questions to stimulate interest, such as, "How many of you feel a special connection with a particular animal? Which one?" Then, "How many of you like one kind of weather better than any other? Which?" (Record some examples on the board.)
2. Say, "In some poems, we say we are the things we like or love. This is a strong comparison called *metaphor*. It's almost as if we could turn ourselves into things we love when we write. We use magic pencils of metaphor! Today's poem is a self-portrait in words. It is also a chant."
3. Have available a copy of "The Delight Song of Tsoai-talee" by N. Scott Momaday. Reproduce it on the worksheet, copy it on chart paper or project. Read to the students; then have them read aloud, too.
4. Ask: "What do you particularly like in the poem?" After some responses, direct attention to the added details about each thing the poet "is." Not just a horse, but "a blue horse that runs in the plain."
5. Return to the animal and weather words you've written on board during step one. Example: "I am a cheetah . . ." Ask the students to add details that give a more precise image of what they like about the cheetah. How do they picture the cheetah in their imaginations? Doing what?
6. Read the student sample poems.
7. Write on the board some categories students might choose from: animals, weather, sounds (music), tastes, a favorite color (and where it's found), and so on.
8. Help students with their writing. Circle the room. Reinforce quiet time.
9. Share the poems after you've given the writers a three-to-five-minute notice to finish.

S. K. The first meeting with a class is so important in establishing a connection with the poet-teacher and an interest in poetry. Before starting with a new group, I obtain a class list and look up the meaning of the first names of each student and the teacher in a names-for-baby book (or www.behindthename.com).
I arrive in class with my small copper dumbek under my arm. This makes me interesting right away.

1. Bring in a rhythm instrument, such as a small hand drum. Pick it up, saying, "All words have rhythm, even our names." Drum your own name, with a strong beat for an accented syllable, a lighter beat for an unaccented one. Say, "Our names are like little poems because they have rhythm and meaning." I tell the students that my name, Susan Kennedy, means "Lily Shining Head."
2. Go down the class list, having each student say their full name. Then drum it, telling them the meaning of their first name and its origins. Have them write this down at the top of a piece of paper they will also use for writing their poems later. The students find this fascinating. They may or may not use the name meaning in their poem, or as the title of it. Still, it's one more way to look at themselves, and spending time on this helps establish a rapport with the class, as well as helping me to learn their names.
3. From this, it's easy to segue into the sample poem, "The Song of Amergin." It arouses student interest, and many of the images correspond with familiar California scenes.

Time and Materials: A rhythm instrument, a class list onto which you have written the meanings of the kids' first names (this takes about an hour to prepare), and a copy of "Delight Song," on a poster, or photocopied, or ready to be projected.

Worksheet

The Song of Amergin
by Amergin, Bard of the Milesians

I am the wind on the sea;
I am the wave of the sea;
I am the bull of seven battles;
I am the eagle on the rock;
I am a flash from the sun;
I am the most beautiful of plants;
I am a strong wild boar;
I am a salmon in the water;
I am a lake in the plain;
I am the word of knowledge;
I am the head of the spear in battle;
I am the god that puts fire in the head;
Who spreads light in the gathering on the hills?
Who can tell the ages of the moon?
Who can tell the place where the sun rests?

(Translated by Lady Augusta Gregory)

Seedling
by Diana Valle, Sonoma County

I am a little dolphin dancing gracefully
    at dusk.
I am a blue bird singing as sweet as honey.
I am a silver doe hiding in the dark.
I am a star shining down at you.
I am the universe rotating the galaxies
    with millions of stars and light and
        the mysteries of life.
I am a seedling sprouting in the earth
alive and ready for a beautiful life.

Panther
by Francisco Nigoa, Sonoma County

I am a black panther that wanders
        the jungle
at midnight and dawn
and runs all day long.
I am a moon that is bright
and I shine in the night.
I am a breeze that cools
down the heat.
I am a bee that wanders
the world at night.
I am an angel that wanders
the heavens and earth, too.

Plantita

*Soy un pequeño delfín graciosamente
    bailando al anochecer.
Soy un pajarito azul cantando dulce
    cual la miel.
Soy una cierva escondiéndose de la oscuridad.
Soy una estrella iluminándote.
Soy el universo girando las galaxias:
    millones de estrellas, luz y
    misterios de la vida.
Soy una plantita brotando de la tierra,
    viva y lista para una vida hermosa.*

(Translated by Diana Valle)

Advice to Writers
Write a poem that is a portrait of you as the things you love or that you find particularly beautiful or meaningful. Start your lines with "I am." Remember to add descriptive information, so we can really see, hear, taste, and experience your favorite things in exactly the way you love them.

Let Us Gather in a Flourishing Way
For Grades Four Through Twelve

by Luis Kong, Ed.D., Director Adult Literacy Services Alameda County Library,
Former Executive Director CPitS, 1990–1995
(based on the poem of the same name by Juan Felipe Herrera)

In the tradition of Walt Whitman and Pablo Neruda, Juan Felipe Herrera's "let us gather in a flourishing way" encourages readers to open their minds and hearts to a culturally diverse landscape by gathering images of family, nature, cultural struggle, and a strong and positive vision of the future. This is a fantastic poem to inspire students to gather ways they view the world and to play with the rhythm of language, both in Spanish and English, while expressing images that reside in their memories and five senses.

Hererra's poem resonates well with fourth and fifth graders, and it can also be inspiring for older kids, including high school students. I would suggest engaging older students in a dialogue about the use of Spanish and English words, and the symbolism expressed by the poet: for example, *turquoise, fields, águila* (eagle), *nopales* (nopal), *maiztlán*, and the juxtaposition of English and Spanish as in *sunluz, hijos rainbows, woven brazos,* and *camino blessing.* Herrera is building a bridge between the two languages and exposing the interior and exterior cultural identities that they represent. This lesson uses repetition, chant, oratory skills, improvisation, and bilingual language practice.

1. Review the students' writings from earlier lessons. Have them read their poems out loud.
2. Tell the students about Juan Felipe Herrera, a California poet, performer, playwright, teacher, and activist. A former farm worker in the Central Valley, in 2012 he was appointed California Poet Laureate. He is currently a professor at the University of California, Riverside.
3. Read Herrera's "let us gather in a flourishing way" aloud. Ask your Spanish-speaking students to talk about what the Spanish words mean to them, for the benefit of students who don't know the language.
4. Discuss the imagery in the poem and the playfulness with language. Discuss rhythm and language. Ask students what are the things that they want to gather, to collect for life. Make a list of words on the board.
5. Write a few sample sentences starting with "Let us gather."
6. Provide at least thirty minutes of writing time.
7. Give the students these ideas for revision: See what words or sentences you'd like to change, move, remove, or replace. Read your poem in reverse starting from the last stanza. How does it sound to you? How does your choice of words in another language give your poem a rhythm? Ask students to consider gathering feelings and other important things. Rewrite.
8. Have students read their new poems aloud.

Materials: In your lesson handout include typed student poems from the previous lesson. If the class is not Spanish-speaking, create vocabulary posters with a variety of words from nature, people, culture, and objects.

Worksheet

let us gather in a flourishing way
by Juan Felipe Herrera

let us gather in a flourishing way
with sunluz grains abriendo los cantos
que cargamos cada día
en el young pasto nuestro cuerpo
para regalar y dar felíz perlas pearls
of corn flowing árboles de vida en las cuatro esquinas
let us gather in a flourishing way
contentos llenos de fuerza to vida
giving nacimientos to fragrant ríos
dulces frescos verdes turquoise strong
carne de nuestros hijos rainbows
let us gather in a flourishing way
en la luz y en la carne of our heart to toil
tranquilos in fields of blossoms
juntos to stretch los brazos
tranquilos with the rain en la mañana
temprana estrella on our forehead
cielo de calor and wisdom to meet us
where we toil siempre
in the garden of our struggle and joy
let us offer our hearts a saludar
our águila rising freedom
a celebrar woven brazos branches ramas
piedras nopales plumas piercing bursting
figs and aguacates
ripe mariposa fields and
mares claros of our face
to breathe todos en el camino blessing
the seeds to give to grow maiztlán
en las manos de nuestro amor

Untitled
*by José Silva Huey,
Sonoma County*

Let us
gather
nuestra
tierra
abandonada
Let the
wild rain
grow our
lazy tree
Let the
trees grow
so the sol
can be excited
otra vez
Let our
bold planet
be proud of
us.

Let us gather
the wind of
anger stay low
deja
nuestros
corazones
be happy.
Let our planeta
be peaceful again.

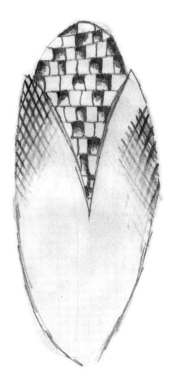

Advice to Writers
Enjoy the sounds of Spanish and English words. Experiment by trying different words next to each other. Make a list of words: ordinary things, places, people. Include the feelings that make you strong, resilient against all odds, that give you a sense of belonging, and make you proud of what you know and have.

Glorious Color Odes
For Grades Four Through Twelve

by Claire Blotter

I never tire of teaching Glorious Color Odes, my favorite lesson, which inspires equally imaginative poems from fourth through twelfth graders. Maybe it's because color awakens students to the power of vivid descriptive details and the visual beauty around them. By praising colors, students learn or practice a range of figurative language: imagery, personification, simile, and metaphor. This lesson works at any time of year, but I like to present it to high schoolers around Valentine's Day, emphasizing that it's not a sexy or muscular body that attracts a true sweetheart but the ability to sensuously enjoy life—and express the wonders of our five senses.

1. Come to class dressed entirely in a favorite color. For middle grades, begin class with "Color Ode Chant" (see the worksheet) to introduce this lesson. For high schoolers, discuss the clichéd symbols of Valentine's Day and how we will examine the power of romantic love and attraction. We will not focus on stereotypical beauty, but find the ability to describe everyday wonders.
2. Briefly introduce Federico García Lorca and Pablo Neruda as two famous Spanish-speaking poets who were passionately involved in life and love and who both wrote amazingly sensual color poems. Neruda's "Ode to Turquoise" is recommended along with the sample poems.
3. Show students a bowl of red fruits and vegetables of different tones and hues. Some may think color is obvious, yet it's actually complex. Ask: "Which apple, tomato, or red pepper is the most red? Notice the tones and hues of blue-red as opposed to yellow-red."
4. Ask: "Can you use words so vividly that they come alive with the same feeling as the color itself?"
5. Ask students to close their eyes, breathe, relax, and imagine a favorite color in their mind's eye. Then, ask them to imagine the different tones of that color in nature, perhaps at the forest or beach, in their clothes, their bedrooms, kitchens, classrooms, etc.
6. Then students share the colors they imagined, and you chose one to brainstorm on the board. Ask for volunteers to contribute variations on specific colors, such as rust, pumpkin, or flame for orange. Students will soon select vivid specific language as you encourage them to think of vegetables, fruits, gems, and parts of nature that exemplify a variety of color tones.
7. Students individually brainstorm names for their own colors, writing and informally sharing them. Circulate among the students, reading aloud especially strong color words you notice so that other students can add them to their lists.
8. Hand out the worksheet and read the Lorca aloud, along with the other sample poems. Read with expression and ask students to echo lines exactly reflecting your vocal intonation. Ask students to point out favorite sensory lines and details to appreciate.
9. On the white board, write a group color poem for the color you brainstormed. Ask students to begin with, "Oh, *Color*," as if they were talking to a character such as *Orange* so that they will experiment with personification. Encourage students to use metaphors in some lines with phrases such as "You are the flaming chile pepper awakening my tongue," and to include some appropriate action words as *kick, leap,* or *run*.
10. Invite students to write their own color poems, using the word list they individually brainstormed and the guidelines above.
11. Circulate around the room as students write, quietly slipping each one an appropriately colored paint swatch. These are easily available in paint stores and display beautiful sensuous color names that students can incorporate into poems.
12. Ask volunteers to share their poems individually, or in a color group alternating lines!

Materials: A bowl of fruits or vegetables of different tones, paint swatches (from paint stores), and your colorful monotoned clothing.

Worksheet

Romance Sonámbulo
(extracto, estrofa una)
  por Federico García Lorca

  Verde que te quiero verde.
Verde viento. Verdes ramas.
El barco sobre la mar
y el caballo en la montaña.
Con la sombra en la cintura,
ella sueña en su baranda,
verde carne, pelo verde,
con ojos de fría plata.
Verde que te quiero verde.
Bajo la luna gitana,
las cosas la están mirando
y ella no puede mirarlas.

Sleepwalker's Lament
(excerpt, first stanza)

  Green, how I want you, green.
Green wind, green limbs.
The ship upon the sea
and the horse on the mountain.
With her waist in shadow,
she dreams from the balcony,
green flesh, green hair,
with eyes of cold silver.
Green, how I love you, green.
Beneath the gypsy moon,
all things are watching her,
and she cannot see them.

  (Translated by Brian Kirven)

Color Ode Chant
  by Claire Blotter, poet-teacher

Today I'm blue. Are you blue, too?
Yesterday I was hot red—
or was that just in my head?
The day before that I was deep green—
or was that in a dream?

Black
  by Tony Dorin, Marin County

Oh black,
You are the one who I feared most as a child.
You made me tremble at night.
Over time I have grown to love and use you
    to my advantage.
Through moonlight you creep and crawl
    through the trees and curtains.
Like a wave of black hawks you raid through
the night and cut through the light
like a stainless-steel knife.
How I wish I could be with you and be as
    dark and cold as you.
Without you I would be covered in light.
Without you I would be weak.
I awake to your anxiety.

Oh, Green
  by Kendall Cormier, Marin County

You are the piece of seaweed
wrapped around a log floating out to sea.
You are the crisp sweet taste
of mint ice cream.
You are the snake that doesn't slither,
you are the mountain that has never been
    climbed.
You are the beautiful dress
of the willow tree.
    Oh, green
You are the shell of the turtle
the juice of the lime.
    Oh, green
You are the go in green light.
You are the calmness of my confusion.
You are the apple doll that made the sorrow
    go away.
You are the trot of the horse, the forest
of my thoughts, the lip of flame.
    Oh, green

Oh, Gray
  by Valentini Muench Mauridoglou, Marin County

You are a wolf's winter coat
You are an old telephone
echoing like driftwood on a white canvas
You are like almonds
getting cracked

California Poets In The Schools

Insecure About Sestinas? (Sestina, Enjambment) For Grades Four Through Twelve

by Phyllis Meshulam

I have been one insecure about sestinas. Then I read "Lunch Bag Sestinas" by Beth Copeland in the Winter 2010–11 issue of *Teachers & Writers*. Copeland's fun/random approach got her students pulling target words out of lunch bags and writing lines to be stitched together later. But she herself admitted that the resulting poems were "more playful than polished." Could I improve on the lesson by making the unit of collaboration the stanza rather than random lines? I was pleased with the results. Use this lesson with students with some previous experience with metaphor and five senses.

1. Look up Elizabeth Bishop's gorgeous poem "Sestina," which is available online. You may want to reproduce all or part of it to give to the class. You will also need to enlarge the template of the form as the one given here is too tiny for classroom use.
2. Depending on how long a residency you have with the students, you may want to select the six end-words for them—based on other writing they've done with you—as I did in the case of these fifth-grade students with whom I had already been writing nature poems.
3. When I did the lesson with juvenile hall students, on the other hand, I had a longer residency and we were able to brainstorm our words together. The main thing is that the six end words should be rich nouns or verbs that all the kids can relate to. The juvie kids had many shared experiences, like lousy food and uniforms, to draw from. Sometimes pairing a final word with an adjective added richness: "stopped clocks," "sidewalk blood." Sometimes these were varied slightly to great effect: "door locks" became "locked doors."
4. Ignore the final thee-line stanza for the main writing session. Insert the pre-selected words in the prescribed order onto your template before making copies for the class.
5. Before students write individually, practice the idea of writing *to* the final word. Make a couple of lines on the board, with a single word at the end of each. Invite volunteers to make up a line that will end with one of those words and *enjamb* (or carry the thought) over onto the next line. This is fun and can make the poem much more interesting. The word comes from French and is related to the word *leg*. I think of someone throwing their leg over a fence to climb over it. Remind the kids that the end of the line is not necessarily the end of the sentence or the thought.
6. Give each student a template with one stanza on it. The kids can be organized into groups of six, but this really isn't necessary. You can stitch the different stanzas together later. (Despite disconnects, the repeated words give a sense of unity and melody.) Remind them to use metaphors, similes, and their five senses.
7. At the end of the class period, it's fun to take six kids, each of whom has written a different stanza in the numbered series, and bring them together at the front of the room. Have them read the newly assembled poem in order.
8. I usually save the writing of the last stanza, or tercet, for a different day. It could be the final day of the residency, when we are doing revisions. I ask for volunteers who would like to take one of the six-stanza poems that I've typed up and create a seventh stanza for it. For this you can use the final part of the template that shows how the six words should be used in three lines, rather than six.

Time and Materials: A copy of Bishop's poem, "Sestina"; an enlarged copy of the template; a pre-session in which to collect the words, either by yourself or in a brainstorming session with the kids. And a post-session in which the final seventh stanza can be written by kids who have seen the first six stanzas typed into a single poem.

Worksheet

Sestina Form

Stanza 1
```
_____ A
_____ B
_____ C
_____ D
_____ E
_____ F
```

Stanza 2
```
_____ F
_____ A
_____ E
_____ B
_____ D
_____ C
```

Stanza 3
```
_____ C
_____ F
_____ D
_____ A
_____ B
_____ E
```

Stanza 4
```
_____ E
_____ C
_____ B
_____ F
_____ A
_____ D
```

Stanza 5
```
_____ D
_____ E
_____ A
_____ C
_____ F
_____ B
```

Stanza 6
```
_____ B
_____ D
_____ F
_____ E
_____ C
_____ A
```

Tercet
```
_____ A _____ B
_____ C _____ D
_____ E _____ F
```

Creek Sestina
by Dane Paulson, Tessla Carlson, Sam Fanucchi, Ana Cruz, and Anna Cline, Sonoma County

The creek by the big redwood,
the creek by the little bridge,
from there you always hear the sound of sticks.
The splash of frogs playing leapfrog.
The tiny creek bed is like a little canyon
with all the wildflowers pollinated by bees.

The gracious, humming bees
gather pollen from the mighty redwood.
The creek sifts through the canyon
where there is no bridge
to pass. Birds playfully join in a game of leapfrog,
while beavers build their homes with sticks.

The wonderful snap of sticks
over the beautiful buzzing sound of honeybees.
The sounds colliding or jumping over each other like leapfrog
or climbing the huge redwood
that stands in their way but they act like it's a bridge.
They make everything seem like a canyon.

The birds soar through the canyon.
The pouring rain makes the sticks crack.
The water whirls beneath the bridge.
Small whispering, humming bees.
There is a tall redwood.
The cranes scream while playing leapfrog.

The water over rocks makes them play leapfrog;
the water echoes like a kid splashing in a canyon.
Then a huge tree growls in the canyon, a redwood.
Every step I take I hear the crunch crunch of sticks.
I see dragonflies chasing bees,
chasing them under the bridge.

The ducks drifting under the bridge,
squirrels jump over branches like playing leapfrog,
the smell of pollen from the bees.
Now the creek hums at the bottom of the canyon.
There are not many more sticks.
There are no more redwoods.

The never-ending redwood forest has darkened. The mystical bridge has closed. The crunch of the sticks. Fish in the creek playing leapfrog. The creek has drifted through the canyon. Now there is a smell of bees.

Advice to Writers

Aim your writing toward the pre-established end word of each line. But don't forget: Your sentence can roll around to the next line! This is called *enjambment*, and it can make your poem more interesting. Remember your magic wand of metaphor, and your five senses.

California Poets In The Schools

Ode to a Quality (Ode, Adjectives, Synesthesia) For Grades Five Through Eight

by Prartho Sereno

A well-written ode, quite simply any poem of praise, is a marvelous thing. Who in this sadly cynical age couldn't use a moment of praise, a fresh reason to say, "Hooray! I'm alive"? But the downfall of odes is how easily they fall into cliché (i.e., automatic, sticky sweet, insincere). This experiment in ode-making takes a counter-intuitive approach by starting in the cool realms of abstraction, then zooming in to the markedly specific and quirkily personal. The process challenges its writers to think metaphorically and to use synesthesia: a deliberate mixing up of the senses that almost always imbues an image with wonder. The model poem, "Pied Beauty," basically an ode to speckled things, has difficult language, but is a marvel to listen to, with all its alliterations and strongly stressed syllables. Encourage students to appreciate the music of this ode to spotted and freckled things.

1. Begin with a class discussion about the *qualities* that make life worth living. We're looking for adjectives that can modify the word *things*. For example, *quiet* (things), *wild* (things). Gather student responses—fill the board with adjectives.
2. A common first response will be obsessions, such as "video games." This creates an opportunity for students to examine the quality that draws them in: *otherworldly, distant, loud,* etc.
3. Stretch the possibilities by including various senses (fuzzy, salty), what things are made of (golden, papery), how they move (twirling, leaping, etc.), their shape (square, flat), condition (worn-out, clean), or beyond the senses (magic, invisible, kind).
4. Give the students a "bubble sheet" with a large inner circle surrounded by at least twelve smaller ones. They will write one quality in the middle bubble along with the word *Things*.
5. Pace the students by asking them to fill the smaller bubbles, one prompt at a time, with specific images that have their quality, including: a) Animal or detail of animal. b) Some detail of a person. c) Emotion or feeling. d) Common object. e) Imaginary things. f) Weather. g) Subject in school. h) Something in the sky. i) Urban details. j) Plant details, including fruits or vegetables.
6. Some questions will be harder for certain qualities, but these generate unique and interesting responses. Encourage metaphorical thinking! And details! Not merely "a pig," but "the curl of a pig's tail," or "a grandfather pig with a scraggly beard." Discourage randomness; instead, tell the poets to shoot for an "aha!" moment, a brand-new connection in their brains!
7. Read the sample poems together, and let the students write their own. They do not need to use everything from their bubble sheets and will hopefully add ideas as they write. I do, however, encourage them to use at least six images from the pre-write, as often we undervalue our brainstorm genius. The great thing about the bubble sheet is that since it imposes no form, students need to find/create their own sense of order.
8. Save at least ten minutes for students to read their work aloud to one another.

Time and Materials: I recommend an hour to allow for sharing. You will need a white board, a bubble sheet for each student, and the worksheet. A wonderful follow-up is to watch a student recitation of the Hopkins poem, which you can find at www.poetryoutloud.org, under "Poems and Performance" and "Watch Video."

Worksheet

Pied Beauty
  by Gerard Manley Hopkins

Glory be to God for dappled things—
   For skies of couple-colour as a brinded cow;
     For rose-moles all in stipple upon trout that swim;
Fresh-firecoal chestnut-falls; finches' wings;
   Landscape plotted and pieced—fold, fallow, and plough;
     And áll trádes, their gear and tackle and trim.

All things counter, original, spare, strange;
   Whatever is fickle, freckled (who knows how?)
     With swift, slow; sweet, sour; adazzle, dim;
He fathers-forth whose beauty is past change:
       Praise him.

Summer—
  by Rene Tolson, Sonoma County

Praise to summer
and all its summery things
with
beautiful butterflies, and
colorful comets
on a starry night
with
wet waterfalls,
green grass, and
the fresh feeling
with
the hot heat.
The days I spend
with
my beloved best friend.
The days under the city lights
in loving Los Angeles,
blasting music
staying up all night
listening to the radio 100.9.
Praise to summer
and all its summery things.

Flying Things
  by Anahi Garcia, Sonoma County

Hooray for flying things.
Clouds that swift through the sky
shaped like unicorns.
Leaves that are like colors forming
throughout the seasons.
Waves that come out from the ocean
and onto land.
Smell of tamales that makes me take flight.
Everything that floats, glides, hops
through the sunset.

Advice to Writers

Go all out in praise of your quality. Convince us (and yourself) of how it spices things up and deepens your experience of being alive. You can (but don't have to) open your poem with one of these:
"I love _____things!"
Or: "I sing the praises of _____things."
Or (hipper): "I'm talkin' 'bout _____things."
Or: "Let me tell you about _____things."
Then start to add your favorite and most surprising ideas from your bubble sheet. Let a few *new* ideas "bubble up," too, and don't forget to wake up your images with specific sensory details.

California Poets In The Schools

If That Picture Could Speak... (Ekphrasis) For Grades Five Through Twelve

by Richard Newsham

If that picture could speak, what tale would it tell you? An act of writing inspired by looking closely at a work of visual art is called *ekphrasis*, a Greek word meaning "to speak out." For over 2,500 years this ancient technique has helped artworks "talk" to us through writers using their full imaginative powers to respond directly to art from the past as well as to artworks by today's creative minds.

1. Give a brief history of ekphrasis. In the 5th century BCE, Homer's "The Shield of Achilles" in the *Iliad* is like a movie screen projecting many scenes: a wedding, trial, army ambush, lion attacking a bull, and dance party. In the 1st century CE, the Latin poet Horace writes: "poetry is a speaking picture" and "a picture is silent poetry." In the 19th century, John Keats talks to a young couple painted on an ancient vase in "Ode on a Grecian Urn" as if they were still alive today (you can find his drawing of the vase on the Internet). Both poetry and visual art speak to our imaginations through the power of images—think of words and language as the poet's or writer's paintbrush.
2. Discuss model poems inspired by art. Project two or three poems and images (from websites below) for students to read aloud, taking turns by stanza. You can mention that a fragment of a statue of Ramses II (aka Ozymandias) in the British Museum inspired Shelley to write his sonnet. For each poem, ask students to say what details they like best, and to identify metaphors and discuss the poet's approach.

Poem & Poet	Artwork
"Ozymandius" by Percy Bysshe Shelley	Photo of Egyptian ruins (see #2 above)
"The Great Figure" by William Carlos Williams	*I Saw the Figure 5 in Gold* by Charles Demeuth
"The Man with the Blue Guitar" by Wallace Stevens	*The Old Guitarist* by Pablo Picasso
"Two Monkeys by Brueghel" by Wislawa Szymborska	*Two Monkeys* by Pieter Brueghel

3. Give students some pre-write ideas as they select (by orderly row or group) from the teacher's stash of images from old art calendars/catalogs, your art museum, or projected on the wall. Say: "Pick an artwork that causes an immediate reaction in you. Then examine it more closely. Look deep inside. Ask yourself: What do I see, feel, or question? Go beyond the story of just describing what is in the artwork. Use all your senses. Make it personal."
4. Ask the students to jot down "writing bubbles" of what immediately strikes them about the artwork: vivid images, details, and metaphors.
5. Say: "Think about how you will make the artwork move as you give the artwork a voice, capture its energy and actions with words, and add your own life or dimension to the artwork."
6. Ask students to create ten to twenty lines of poetry or a minimum of five sentences full of imagination, colors, and metaphors.
7. Allow time for students who want to read aloud their creations.

Time and Materials: Sixty to seventy minutes to discuss, write, and share; paper or laptops to write on; a white board and projector for sample poems, handouts, and images (or use old art calendars/catalogs). Visit these ekphrastic poetry websites to view all model and worksheet images and poems:
  http://www.english.emory.edu/classes/paintings&poems/titlepage.html
  http://www.cityofventura.net/arttales 2013 images inspired the two student worksheet poems.

Worksheet

Ozymandias
by Percy Bysshe Shelley

I met a traveller from an antique land
Who said: Two vast and trunkless legs of stone
Stand in the desert. Near them, on the sand,
Half sunk, a shattered visage lies, whose frown,
And wrinkled lip, and sneer of cold command,
Tell that its sculptor well those passions read
Which yet survive, stamped on these lifeless things,
The hand that mocked them, and the heart that fed;
And on the pedestal these words appear:
"My name is Ozymandias, king of kings:
Look on my works, ye Mighty, and despair!"
Nothing beside remains. Round the decay
Of that colossal wreck, boundless and bare
The lone and level sands stretch far away.

Mojave
(inspired by Mojave *by Dorothy Hunter)*
 by Dahyun Na, Contra Costa County

Another wrinkle next to my eye
Disturbance under my misty, barren surface
Remembering my past
My heart not yet fully healed
Bubbling with confusion of mixed colors
Forced into one place
Like oil and water that never seem to mix
Red love for my home
Red passion for my tribe
Orange liveliness in traditions from my ancestors
Orange fascination in growth of my children
Green joy in peaceful, repeated daily routine

Orange warning for strangers who harm Mother Nature
Red rage toward invaders who took away my home
Dark blue powerlessness
like falling through an endless tunnel with no exit
Orange loneliness in a new environment without my family
Yellow hope for the return of my old life
Perplexities under my smooth surface
Living my life with memories, carrying the past

Blue Trees
(inspired by Blue Trees *by Richard Amend)*
 by Nadia Connelly, Ventura County

Soft sunshine shines
through our branches.
The soft grass sways
as if dancing in the wind.

The sun is as brilliant
as a bonfire in the sky.
Silver deer gallop so fast
it is as if they are flying.

Wicked smiles are carved
onto our trunks.
We are the keepers
of the forest.

Squirrels scamper
quickly up our trunks
tickling us
with their big, bushy tails.

Sounds of lonely bird cries
echo off us
filling the silent forest
with sound.

The smell of crisp leaves
fills our noses.
The hot sun shines
and makes us warm.

But the soft whispery wind
sings its song
and cools us
charming every animal.

If we are quiet
you can hear
every animal's heart beating.
We are all united.

Advice to Writers
Here are a few of ways to "get write inside" your artwork. *Create your own story about the painting. Answer the question: "What is going on?" *Make the artwork speak. Create a conversation or argument among the people or even objects depicted.*Enter the artwork yourself—climb inside the picture—and describe your experiences.*Pretend you are the artist. What's on your mind as you work?

California Poets In The Schools

Inspired by the Chinese (Shi) For Grades Seven Through Twelve

by Susan Herron Sibbet (adapted by Phyllis Meshulam)

When the rains start to give way to bright sunshine, and the eighth graders have really gotten into their love poems and deep poems and silly poems, sometimes it's fun to bring in branches of blossoms and break away from the usual format of writing wildly after looking at older poets' poems. Instead, I say, "Let's learn about a very old form."

Many of my students are second-generation American-born Chinese here at this farthest-west school district in San Francisco, the closest to China. Many threads draw together in this exercise, which uses Chinese characters to begin the discussion of the image.

I begin this class by talking about the Chinese language, and how I was always interested in its beauty. I tell of my sister born in China, of our family having to leave in the war, and how I grew up fascinated with the beauty of the written characters I saw on books or prints or games we had brought with us.

1. Pass out the worksheet, which has a few Chinese characters on it. You can talk about how these shapes aren't the sounds of the words but the actual representation of their meaning.
2. The worksheet also includes Poem 12, from Angel Island, the detention center in the middle of San Francisco Bay, where thousands of young men and women were forced to wait under the Chinese Exclusion Act (1882–1943) before they were allowed to come into this country. They had to prove they were "paper sons": that they were related to families already here.
3. Explain what these people did during all the days and weeks and months while they waited: They carved poems into the walls, poems that were found just before the buildings were to be torn down after being abandoned for thirty years.
4. Read, or have students read, the translation of Poem 12 on the worksheet. Be sure everyone knows that the vernal equinox is the first day of spring.
5. Ask: "What would it be like seeing spring arrive around you on the island? In spring, mists, fogs, and storms leave the bay, and San Francisco shines before you—but you cannot go there. What might this have looked like to these detainees, all times of day? What might they have heard?"
6. Have students look closely at the characters for *heart*, for *autumn*, and for *sadness*, included on the worksheet. Point out how the character for *sadness* is really a composite of *heart* and *autumn*. Ask: "How does that make you feel about Poem 12's last line?" ("It is spring but I am feeling the sadness of autumn in my heart.")
7. If you can, bring in some translations (and the originals) of ancient Chinese Shi poems. Many of the Angel Island writings were modeled after these short poems, usually no more than ten lines long, with four to seven characters per line. If you are lucky enough to have Chinese speakers in the classroom, they could read aloud some of these tightly constructed poems, some of which even read in two directions, something like an acrostic. This form seems to have originated during the Eastern Zhou dynasty, around 700—400 BCE, in the Spring and Autumn period.
8. Be sure to save time for a discussion, which can become quite impassioned, about immigration in general. How fair were these laws? (Note that the Exclusion Act was repealed during World War II so the Chinese immigrants could help fight.) What about immigration today? Why do people want to come to California?
9. Choose kids to read the student poems.
10. Write! Share!

Materials: The following books may enrich the discussion: *Island* by Him Mark Lai, Genny Lim, and Judy Yung (University of Washington Press, 1980, 2014); *You Can Write Chinese*, by Kurt Wiese (Viking, 1973); *Lipo and Tu Fu*, ed. Arthur Cooper (Penguin, 1973).

Worksheet

Poem 12
*by an anonymous detainee
from Angel Island Detention Center*

Today is the last day of winter,
Tomorrow morning is the vernal equinox.
One year's prospects have changed to another.
Sadness kills the person in the wooden building.

(Translated by Genny Lim in Island *)*

The Emigrant
by Brian Lee, San Francisco County

There is a man
He walks through the still night
He can see the moon shine brightly on the bay
Through mist and fog a city emerges
He can hear the city still alive
He thinks of what lies ahead
And if he will ever get that far

Chinese Characters

The Strange Weather
by Alice Truong, San Francisco County

This morning as I awoke,
I heard this beautiful chirping
noise made by a small little bird.
The little bird trying to hide from
the pouring rain which
made splashing noises.

Through the day the weather changed from bad to worse
rain dropping like a powerful
waterfall

The clouds as fierce as
a lion. Black darkening
clouds which made rain
pour like crazy

The beginning of Spring
which made the season
special. Spring would
never be the same.

 Heart

 Autumn

 Sad

Advice to Writers
Imagine yourself on that island, or imagine a time when you wished you could be somewhere else and had no way to get there. Imagine where you are: I am . . . I see, smell, hear, feel . . . My surroundings are . . .
Imagine where you wish you could be: in/on/at . . .
Here are some starters you might want to try:
This place calls me, tells me . . .
When I am there, I will . . .
Unfairness is (or is like) . . .

California Poets In The Schools

Riddles for All Ages

by Emmanuel Williams

Riddles appear in the Bible, the Koran, and in ancient Sanskrit and Norse manuscripts. Shakespeare, Swift, Schiller, Goethe, Poe, Jane Austen, Lewis Carroll, and Tolkien all wrote riddles. Students of all ages enjoy riddles. They can be used to get kids writing for the sheer love of challenging others, or they can be used to illustrate a range of forms and techniques: rhyme, metaphor, repetition, word-blends, alliteration, homographs, and so on. I've arranged the riddles below with this in mind (however, for younger students I suggest you simply do riddles for their own sake). Riddles, more than any other kind of writing, are inherently social. When you've written one, you want to see if it works.

1. Explain to the students that a riddle is a word puzzle in which you try to guess the subject. Most riddle subjects talk of themselves without giving their names, so you have to look at the details provided and work out what's speaking.
2. Jump right into a riddle: *I grow in your garden / I glow in your room / Only the name is the same.* Let students guess for a while, offering some hints and repeating the riddle as necessary: "It's something that grows outside—not a seed, because that doesn't glow in a room. Maybe it's a word with two meanings." Answer: a bulb. It's important to get a sense of how long to let the students keep guessing and when to give them the answer and move on.
3. Tell the students you're going to try another riddle that works in a different way: *A maiden lives in a high green house / Her tears are red as blood, but her heart is a stone.* Again, offer hints and repeat the riddle as necessary. "What does *high, green house* make you think of? A tree? Yes. So it's something that lives, or grows, in a tree. A fruit? Good—what kind of fruit?" Answer: a cherry or a plum.
4. Pass out the worksheet and explain that it has several more riddles. Share one of them right now, No. 3, which uses rhyme. Read it or have one of the students do so. Then call on students as they come up with answers. Repeat questions and offer hints as above. Answer: footprints.
5. For younger students, I tell them to ignore headings such as *metaphor* and *assonance*. Ask a student to read the first riddle, which makes use of metaphor. Using the model above, offer hints and call on students as they guess the subject. When a student gets the right answer, ask the class to write it in below the riddle. Repeat this formula with a few other riddles on the worksheet. (Answers: 1. toothbrush, 2. snowman, 3. footprints, 4. ocean wave, 5. ring, 6. fire extinguisher.) Repeat with the other riddles, as time allows.
6. Now it is time to try writing a class riddle. Say, "Let's try writing a riddle together. The clues should be fair but tricky. If you were going to write a riddle about a clock, and you wrote: *I go tick-tock,* then you've made it too easy. But if you say something like *I have a face, but no mouth / I have hands, but no fingers,* then you're creating a mystery. So, someone give us a subject— something ordinary, familiar—and we'll make up a riddle about it." As students throw out possible subjects, I look for something that would lend itself to a riddle and that all the students would know. As we create the riddle together, I write the lines on the board and ask for feedback on suggestions: "Was that hint too easy, too hard?" and so on.
7. Now it is time for them to write their own riddles. Tell them they can write riddles about almost anything. The riddles don't have to rhyme but if a student wants to write a rhyming riddle, that's fine.
8. Leave plenty of time for the students to read their riddles and for other students to guess the answers!

Materials: Board or chart paper. Optional: *Riddles Ancient and Modern* by Mark Bryant (Peter Bedrick Books); *A World Treasury of Riddles* by Phil Cousineau (Conari Press); *Riddles,* a pack of forty-eight of my riddles, available from Pomegranate Communications, and my *365 Riddles,* available as an app for the iPad and iPhone.

Worksheet

No. 1 (metaphor)
by Emmanuel Williams, poet-teacher

My body is long;
my head is a clump of stiff strong stalks.
Every morning, and every evening
I wear a soft hat, I enter the cave
and dance across white stones,
making them sparkle.

Answer:_____

No. 2 (repetition)
by Emmanuel Williams, poet-teacher

I am a man without bones, my flesh is white
I am a man without blood, my flesh is cold
I am a man without life, my flesh is shrinking
I am the man you made and lost.

Answer:_____

No. 3 (rhyme)
by Emmanuel Williams, poet-teacher

I show the world that you were here.
Sometimes I'm hard to see
sometimes I'm clear.
I show your skip, your jump, your run
and when the rain descends
I'm quickly gone.

Answer:_____

No. 4 (assonance and alliteration)
by Emmanuel Williams, poet-teacher

Long have I wandered
The wide ways of the whale, and the wild wind.
Storm stirred me; calm caressed me;
The sun and moon spread gold and silver
Across my glossy back.
Now the wanderer's long salt song
Is near complete. Here at my quest's end
I tilt tall, break and tumble
White slide hissing at your hopping feet.

Answer: _____

No. 5
by Jack Broome, San Mateo County

My heart is of the hardest stone,
my body soft yet sculpted.
Left alone there is no love
but together I create the unbreakable bond.

Answer: _____

No. 6
by Jack Broome, San Mateo County

I am your guardian and shield against
  catastrophe.
You may never use me yet you may owe me
  your life.
My brothers and sisters sit idle with
different organs in all our fiery glory.

Answer: _____

Prompts
Here's a list of subjects to choose from if you're stuck: dog, umbrella, tattoo, river, locker, basketball, baseball mitt, volcano, mirror, eagle, ashes, mermaid, backpack, fountain, wig, spaghetti, hair dryer, match, earwig, rainbow, harp, memory, cross, rumor, eraser, doll, frost, phoenix, alphabet, soap, whale, comb, curtain, eyelid, hamburger, bomb, bee, fingerprint, bike, pencil, juggler, cave, stomach, fan, shoe, glasses, teeth, snake, seesaw, fingernails, sponge, circle, box, lullaby, sleeve, eye, egg, diaper, fireworks, garbage can.

California Poets In The Schools

Poetry in the Science Class (Rhyme, Couplets, Metaphor) For Grades Seven Through Twelve

by Kathy Evans (adapted by Phyllis Meshulam)

Basho once said that if you look long enough at something you will see a hidden glimmering there. I suppose that is what the scientist and the poet have in common. Both, if they are attentive to their world, look for the hidden glimmerings in things.

Most of what comes to us through formal education is diced up into chunks and bite-sized pieces. We have semesters, departments, periods, chapters, and usually seven tidy subjects a day, so I like the idea of fusing disciplines. Some years ago, I was invited to teach poetry in a biology class and did so for several years, which is how this lesson came to be.

1. Find a copy of "Lamb," by Michael Dennis Browne. It was published in Robert Bly's *News from the Universe* and is available online. Read this poem to the students. The speaker of the poem witnesses the birth of a lamb. Initiate a discussion of how both poetry and biology share an awe of creation and new life, and value the simple act of seeing and, hopefully, at some moment, the *eureka!* of imagination.
2. Another poem that budding biologists and poets enjoy is Arthur Guiterman's "Ode to the Amoeba," reprinted on the worksheet. Written in couplets during the Depression, its zany rhymes and cleverness will appeal to students. And you can use this as a moment to talk about what a couplet is.
3. Brainstorm some of the scientific vocabulary that the kids have acquired by now and write the words on the board or on chart paper, so they will be reminded to use them as they write.
4. Read the sample poems on the worksheet, appreciating the unusual rhymes. Try a few of these as a group. Ask: "What would you choose to rhyme with "flagellum?" If you have a rhyming dictionary in your bag of tricks, you can demonstrate how it works and let it circulate during writing time.
5. Mention how both poetry and science pay attention to analogies, which we usually call *metaphors* or *similes* in poetry. How are dissimilar things alike in some mysterious way? How does each shed light on the other? There are many poems you could bring in to illustrate this phenomenon in poetry. "Free Union," a metaphor-rich description of his wife, by André Breton, is one.
6. Science teachers tend to be thrilled when students make these associations. When one of her students wrote, "The amoeba is like a transparent milkshake, cytoplasm flowing like water from a faucet, food particles passing through the cell membrane like a ghost through a wall . . . ," one practically shrieked with joy. She said with amazement, "Yes, yes, that's exactly what it does!" Poet-teachers will be joyous, too!
7. Turn the students loose to write about something they have become familiar with in science class. Encourage them to use some science vocabulary as well as metaphors.
8. Share!

Materials: A copy of the poem "Lamb"; to illustrate metaphor, the section on his wife from "Free Union" by André Breton; lists of science vocabulary recently taught to the class. Optional: A rhyming dictionary or two could be fun.

Worksheet

Ode to the Amoeba
by Arthur Guiterman

Recall from Time's abysmal chasm
That piece of primal protoplasm
The First Amoeba, strangely splendid,
From whom we're all of us descended.
That First Amoeba, weirdly clever,
Exists today and shall forever,
Because he reproduced by fission;
He split himself, and each division
And subdivision deemed it fitting
To keep on splitting, splitting, splitting;
So, whatsoe'er their billions be,
All, all amoebas still are he.
Zoologists discern his features
In every sort of breathing creatures,
Since all of every living species,
No matter how their breed increases
Or how their ranks have been recruited,
From him alone were evoluted.
King Solomon, the Queen of Sheba
And Hoover sprang from that amoeba;
Columbus, Shakespeare, Darwin, Shelley
Derived from that same bit of jelly.
So famed is he and well-connected,
His statue ought to be erected,
For you and I and William Beebe
Are undeniably amoebae!

Ode to a Volvox
by David Weiskoph, Marin County

Recall way, way back to the Volvox,
to the colors of its rolling box.
How lucky it doesn't have to pay the bill,
for it has, inside and out, its own chlorophyll.
It moves in a fashion which is mellow,
the Volvox does this with its flagellum.
When the Volvox gets the urge,
the Volvox has a splitting surge.
It splits and splits and splits, and then,
the whole colony system starts again.

Note: A volvox is a protozoan colony of cells rolling together in a sphere.

Planaria
by Chris Dunnibier, Marin County

My Planaria—with a head like a triangle
   with eyespots like saucers
     staring back at me;
my Planaria with a pharynx like a rubber band
   sitting patiently with its cilia
     beating like a conveyor belt;
my Planaria with its pigment spots regenerating
   like freckles, with its gastrovascular cavity
     dissolving like a glutton;
my Planaria, complete now, long and skinny,
   like an old finger in a petri dish.

Note: A planaria is a free-swimming freshwater flatworm.

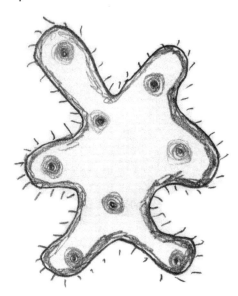

Advice to Writers
Help yourself to some of the science vocabulary we wrote on the board. Make metaphors, similes, and analogies to shine a new light on your subject. If you want, you can experiment with finding rhymes for some of the odd scientific words.

Mostly for Older

Playing with Sound Strategies (Assonance, Consonance, and Rhyme) For Middle School and High School Students

by Jennifer Swanton Brown

Poetry is different from other types of writing in part because of the way sound is used to convey meaning. This is a hard concept for young writers to understand, and as a result, it's often left out of lessons. Young writers do respond, however, to sound strategies when presented as play. A lesson that invites students to "goof around with sound" may seem superficial or "too easy," but the results often reveal much about a writer's inner thoughts. And the writing is definitely fun. This lesson starts with a playful, rather odd-ball poem, moves into simple rhyme games, and then launches a poem of self-discovery.

1. Read the poem "Girl Sleuth" out loud to the class (don't pass it out yet). Instruct students to listen to the way the poem sounds, more than worrying about what it means. Tell them to write down any words on their paper that catch their attention.
2. Ask for volunteers to call out what words they heard, liked, and remembered. Write them on the board.
3. Pass out the poem and read it aloud again. Have students circle interesting words on the page this time.
4. Working on the board, have students identify words that sound similar:
   - Words that rhyme: *drew, blue, clue, too, 1962; Brenda, pretenda*
   - Words with similar consonant sounds (consonance): *secret, locket, cactus, click-click, raincoats, sticks*
   - Words with similar vowels sounds (assonance): *girl, bird, word, shkrrrr; read, seeds, gleam, beak, she*
5. (Optional) Briefly outline the poem's "action": a young girl hides, reading near cactus, birds in late summer; Nancy Drew was a fictional girl detective about whose books (yellow/blue-covered) the young Brenda has written a report in 1962; can Nancy find the "brenda/pretenda" character from the dress and locket clues? *Stress that this is not a poem with deep complicated meaning, but a poem of memory, investigation, and discovery.*
6. Have students write their names on their papers and come up with rhymes. (This can be done as a group, watching out to discourage nasty or teasing rhymes.)
7. Have students remember a hiding place from childhood, or a favorite book or song. Instruct them to make rhyme lists for those numbers and titles. (This step can also be done on the board as a group.)
8. Instruct students to write a poem about their remembered place and/or book or song. Give them the usual instructions to use all their senses and use plenty of verbs and concrete description. Encourage them to use their own name and its rhyme, if that works out. Let them write for fifteen minutes.
9. Now, have students pick words at random from their poems and make rhyming lists from those words. The point is to use sound to suggest different word choices, rather than meaning. Surprises will happen! *This is the crux of the lesson.*
10. Use rhyming dictionaries and lists to revise poems, rather than thesauruses. Invent words as needed, such as *pretenda* and *shkrrrr*).

Materials: Rhyming dictionaries.

Worksheet

Girl Sleuth
  by Brenda Hillman

A brenda is missing—where is she?
Summon the seeds & weeds, the desert whooshes. Phone the finch
with the crowded beak; a little pretenda
  is learning to read
in the afternoon near the cactus caves. Near oleander & pulpy
caves with the click-click of the wren & the shkrrrr of the thrasher,
  a skinny pretenda is learning
to read till the missing brenda
  is found. Drip of syllables like olives near the saguaro.
Nancy Drew will find the secret in raincoats & wednesdays
  & sticks. Nancy whose spine is yellow
  or blue will find the brenda in 1962,
Nancy   who has no mother,
  who takes suggestions from her father & ignores them.

Gleam goes the wren ignoring the thorn. They cannot tell the difference.
Click of the smart dog's nails on linoleum.
  Nancy bends over the clues,
of brenda's locket & dress. Word by word
  between syllables a clue. Where has the summer gone, the autumn—
are they missing too? Maybe Nancy
  will parse the secret & read the book report on Nancy Drew:
"neat pretty sly cute." Syllable by syllable
  & still no brenda! Nancy
puts her hand to her forehead; is the missing
girl in the iron bird? is the clue to the girl in the locket?

Advice to Writers

1. *Move your arm.* When you start writing, *keep going*— even if you aren't sure about what you're saying. Poems come from your body, from the words slipping out the end of your pencil or pen on the page. Poems come from words, not from ideas waiting in your head.

2. *The answer to every question is "Yes."* If you have a question about your poem, it's a good bet that your teacher will say it's okay to try. Go ahead and try!

Poems for Paintings
For High School Students

by Duane BigEagle

I like to begin a poetry workshop with *imagery*. As a painter, it comes naturally to me to use paintings as a source for imagery. As a Native American (Osage Tribe), I like to proceed from the concrete to the abstract, and this works well with most children (ages four to ninety-four). This exercise has ensured successful poetry workshops for over thirty years.

1. First, I ask students what *imagination* is. After some discussion, we usually arrive at the idea that imagination is our ability to "make something up" (a lie is the worst use of imagination).
2. Next, I ask students what the root word of *imagination* is (a word grows out of its roots, just as a tree does), and eventually they come up with the word *image*. I tell them that scientists have discovered that about 89 percent of human beings have visual imaginations, meaning that when our imagination works, it most often appears in the mind first as a visual image, though for some it may be a sound or a smell.
3. An image is a picture; for writers, it's a picture made with words. But how do you make a good image? Is it a good image if I say: "There's a horse in a field"? What about if I say: "There's a wild white Arabian stallion thundering across a green field scattered with orange poppies"? Of course the second one is better, and we learn that a good image contains details—I like to say at least three details.
4. Next, I tell them of my love of painting and say I'd like to get started with imagery by giving them an image/painting to make over again in words. I always give a couple of examples of what I'm looking for: the first from a painting called *Sunset at Ivry* by the French painter Armand Guillaumin. I show them the painting and ask them to come up with lines. If there's any hesitation, I ask them what time of day is in the painting and let that be the first line. On the worksheet is the "beginner's" poem that I wrote for this landscape painting of a city with a river and fields. You can make one up for another painting.
5. "Tahitian Women" may be best for older students. It shows how even a short poem can talk about complex human relationships.
6. I collect calendars of paintings and cut them up to give each student four to five choices. French Impressionists and Japanese wood-block artists like Hiroshige and Hokusai work best because of good details. Artists like Romare Bearden, Jacob Lawrence, Salvador Dalí, René Margritte, and Georgia O'Keeffe can work well for follow-up lessons.
7. As the students begin to write, I remind them, "Look for details. Use modifying words: 'tan gravel path' is better than just 'path.' Use colors." (A painting has colors!)
8. I point out that phrases like "In the painting there is . . ." are probably unnecessary. I ask them just to tell me what they see, to make a picture for the reader.
9. After they've been writing for about five minutes, I remind them to use their five senses. I ask them: if they were in the painting, what sounds would they hear? Can they put a sound in their poem? What smells? What textures? Even "cotton candy clouds" can be descriptive and interesting!
10. With about eight to ten minutes left in the writing period, I ask them to tell the story behind the painting and suggest that even a simple landscape painting can have a story—is it the coming of evening or the coming of winter? I also tell them that a title can be an important line in a poem and can sometimes tell the story. A painting of two people walking on a beach was given a story because of the title, *The Wedding Proposal*.

Materials: Calendars of paintings, cut up to allow each student to have a few choices. A projection of the paintings described in the model poems or your own poem for a painting you have.

Worksheet

The City at Evening
(*for* Sunset at Ivry *by Armand Guillaumin*)
  by Duane BigEagle, poet-teacher

Across the bend in the slow-moving river,
dark factories puff gray smoke
into an orange and yellow evening sky,
which fades to turquoise as the sun sets.
Stately white houses stand guard on the opposite shore,
waiting to greet their owners with the smell of dinner.
A lonely brown farmhouse
resting on an island in the middle of the river
is shaded by tall green poplar trees on a small hill.
The sounds of factory whistles and grinding gears
creep across the quiet river,
attacking the peacefulness of autumn fields.
The river becomes a mirror, catching
the last glowing lights from the sky
as evening settles in.

Tahitian Women
(*for a painting by Paul Gauguin*)
  by Duane BigEagle

It's lovely to be languorous
at the end of the day
when the breeze begins to blow
from across the blue lagoon.
Yes, it's fine to sit on the warm sand
with a friend,
speak of things
important and unimportant,
perhaps to share a pipe of tobacco
according to their custom.
The woman in pink
without looking
twists a small bit of marsh grass
into a rope.
But how curious
they've both come to sit
on either side
of the small white flower
dropped
earlier in the day
when the one
went walking
with the other one's husband.

Advice to Writers
Things you should include in your image poem:
- What is the time of day/time of year? This gives you an easy first line and gets you started.
- Describe the background next: what's the sky like, or, if inside, what are the walls like? Details!
- In the main part of the painting, what do you see?
- If people are involved, give at least one detail: "the boy in the red jacket."
- Look for other details: what will make a picture in the reader's mind?
- What's the story behind the painting? What has happened, or what's going to happen?

We Believe in Poetry
For Middle School and High School

by Tobey Kaplan (inspired by CPitS colleague Karin Faulkner)

I believe a leaf of grass is no less than the journey-work of the stars...
  —Walt Whitman, "Song of Myself"

I like to view poetry as the examination of beliefs or tenets, what ideas we hold dear in the forms of statements and images. Poetry saves us again and again; it is the container for the disparities of our lives. Through imaginative language, we explore the contradictions of shared human experience, emotions, ambitions, perceptions, or attitudes, so that any poem is a process of creative discovery and collective empowerment. I believe that poetry connects us to people from all times and cultures.

Here's the plan for middle school students and older:

1. "Shout-out": Brainstorm a series of beliefs as a list on the white board. It's good to get some of the obvious ones out of the way first, so I recommend mentioning to the class that this isn't an exercise for religious conversation or conversion (belief in God, Santa Claus, Jesus, grandmother, and so on). Instead it's about what we like, what we notice, what we remember, the details of the lives that compose us: the core of who each of us might be as a person, as in what observation or experience has remained a part of your personality or sensibility. Share the Whitman quote above, as well as "I have always depended on the kindness of strangers" (Blanche DuBois in Tennessee Williams's *A Streetcar Named Desire*). We believe in the taste of our grandmother's chicken soup, the dog whose sleeping breath is our poem—something that we like to remember.

2. Write down whatever the students speak out and share it out loud: "Trees are giants watching over the land." Or "The eye of the storm is the curiosity of children." Or "The light frightens darkness." Keep the energy flowing and random while creating a group poem in this way.

3. We can move students into the philosophical realm while creating an image-based poem. One suggestion is to lead a discussion based on this question: What has America stood for throughout its history? How has it lived up to those ideals, and how has it failed to? Share the poem "America" by Claude McKay with the students here. McKay is a well-known poet of the Harlem Renaissance, who despite being excluded from many creative arenas because of his Afro-Jamaican ethnic heritage, still believed in the promise of this country, as seen in this poem, published in 1921. Notice how he uses concrete details to show how he feels conflicted: "the bread of bitterness," "tiger's tooth" in his neck, the "bigness" like a flood.

4. Remind students to use the vocabulary of the five senses expressed through nouns and verbs rather than labeling experience using adjectives. Ask them to focus on descriptions of place and the material world of weather, seasons, and geography, and to juxtapose those or arrange them with straightforward statements of actions or activity. Encourage them to remain playful with words and syntax, and to move words around to create surprises.

5. Tell your students: "You can think of this poem as an image list or as an arrangement/juxtaposition of images and statements; you can focus on one place or several places; you can describe something obvious, introduce philosophy and politics; or state something that seems crazy, wild, or extraordinary."

6. Read my poem "Self-Portrait as a Sky Diver," then let the students run with it on their own.

Materials: "America," by Claude McKay, available on the Internet. Some other choices, also found online: "Let America Be America Again" (1933), by Langston Hughes, expresses similar ideas and sentiments to McKay's poem; Mary Oliver's poem "Wild Geese" (1985) reminds us of our shared longing, desperation, and need for connection to one another and the natural world.

Worksheet

Self-Portrait as a Sky Diver
(excerpt)
  by Tobey Kaplan

My vocabulary is groundless
in the lovely distance of tool sheds where ghosts shine at night;
gaps in the air, griddled streets, consequences of music
the modern condition of dust . . .
do any of us know how we are related,
our lives passing through one another like air?
In the expanse of blue, love is an anchor and a mast.
The opening of gentle wind, violet sky, trembling stars.
Kids say the clouds look like cotton;
I say the words are clouds inside the wounds of our hearts,
and the baby's breath of sweet light
washes the bitterness out of my mouth . . .
trains ribbon the landscape;
dancers and businessmen enter the railroad cars
and pass by little church towns and the horns toot into nightfall . . .
Fast and cheap steaming food
thickly layered, collision, fragments, variety
necessary and helpful neighbors
footprints underground surface.
As the air presses like a sword . . .
The most precious gift is doubt.
Or maybe curiosity, after all . . .
Kids at sixteen with casual despair of small talk,
painfully honest with sweaty palms . . .
I'm lucky, but unsure what to order.
A stone wears the embrace of a wave . . .
the curve of Earth . . .

Advice for Writers

- Use the vocabulary of the five senses expressed through nouns and verbs rather than labeling experience by using adjectives.
- Remain playful with words and syntax.
- Move words around to create surprises.

Imagery, Fantasy, and Freedom (Imagery, Narrative) For Grades Seven and Up

by Tresha Faye Haefner

Kids love to think about the freedom they will have as adults: the things they will be able to do, and the things they won't have to do anymore, what they will become, and what their lives will be like. In this exercise, you can help kids get clearer about their fantasy futures by showing them how to create a more powerful scene with imagery.

1. Ask students whether they know what the word *imagery* means.
2. Explain/review that imagery is language that captures and reminds us of what we see, hear, taste, touch, or smell. Add a couple of examples from public domain literature, or from your own work.
3. Have students make a class list of some of the many things in the room that could be captured in imagery, making a separate list for each of the five senses.
4. Explain to students that imagery is an important part of poetry because it helps the reader really see and feel what the writer is trying to show them.
5. Read together Tresha Faye Haefner's poem "When I Move to the Mountains." (You may also want to show them "A Warning" by Jenny Joseph, or "Marcus Millsap: School Day Afternoon" by Dave Etter.)
6. Ask for examples of imagery in Haefner's poem. You could even add them to more than one of your lists of the five senses. For example, "dirt under my fingernails" could be both sight and touch.
7. Point out that the poet uses imagery to show things she likes and things she doesn't like. Give some examples.
8. Read Nathan's poem and ask for images that also stand out.
9. Ask students to write their own poems of at least twenty lines in which they describe what they will do when they get older (alternatively, you may ask them to describe what life will be like when they have some other wish fulfilled, such as "When I get my new dirt bike I will . . . ," or "When it is my birthday I will . . .").
10. Instruct them to use imagery that appeals to several of the five senses.
11. Challenge them to use at least one example of imagery that describes something they do not like. (Sometimes it is helpful to have students write down one thing they do not like before you assign the poem. Then instruct them to find a way to incorporate imagery of the unfavorable thing into the poem about the fulfillment of their wishes.)
12. Note that the theme has a tendency to inspire narrative-type poems, in which a story is told. This can be a good way to reinforce the writing of narrative in other parts of the curriculum.

Time and Materials: This assignment can take an entire class period. You will need pens, paper, the worksheet and copies of any other sample poems, a white board, chart paper, and markers.

Worksheet

When I Move to the Mountains
(after Jenny Joseph)
 by Tresha Haefner

I will live in a log cabin with a patch of sunflowers out front,
and wear a hat full of holes and boots the color of mud,
and have long braids down my back and own a dog named Max
and drive an ugly blue pickup truck through town.
At night I'll boil potatoes in an old dented pot
and read books that nobody else reads anymore
and sit in a calico chair covered with doilies and listen
to the sound of snow out my window,
and drink plain coffee and squint at the sun and say things to my neighbors
like "howdy" and "nice to meetcha" and "hi."
Most of my education will be lost and I will wander around town
not knowing things about the Renaissance
or how they used to put egg yolks in paint to make it stick,
or how to find the square root of anything.
Instead I will learn a lot about the price of wood and the weight of eggs
how long it is till the dead of winter and which is the shortest day of spring.
I will buy groceries on credit and borrow books from the library
and make dresses out of gingham and blankets out of wool.

And get old and fat and have a head like a snow globe
and a belly like a frozen grape and laugh at little things
like birds picking worms out of my garden path,
and cats playing on my living room rug.

And when it gets cold, I will buy an old ugly coat
and a heater for the truck and a dog sweater for Max.
And in the spring when I start to dig and get dirt under my fingernails
I will remember everything about the first day of school
the cleanness of my uniform, the sharp edges of my desk
and I'll smile, and leave it there.

A Day in My Ideal Life
 by Nathan Mosher, L.A. County

When I wake up, a dog,
or a woman, or both
will be at my bedside.
The shower's already on.
My jacket's skewed
a little to the left,
and my shoes battered
but still expensive. The
woman is still asleep.

We will walk, on the sidewinding
streets of San Francisco. Mostly up,
and when down, the dog strays
and wanders. But we make it
to the coffee shop. The coffee shop,
the one and only. Setting my stuff
down on the run-down couch,
the barista gives me
the usual.

The couch feels warm and
homeless and my laptop is
expensive. Then I write,
in my notebook or laptop,
sometimes chatting
with random people I have
seen many times but refuse to
indulge more than just
a *Hey you, how have you
been?*

But I will write, then
perform at night in an obscure
place where people do not
know my name. The lights shine
on their faces and darken my shadow.
And somehow,
I'm not poor.

Advice to Writers
Remember to use lots and lots of imagery. Try to use at least one example of imagery for each of your five senses. But most of all, have fun and enjoy!

Crisis in the Classroom (Juxtaposition) For Middle School and High School

by Karin Faulkner

Twice in one school year when I was checking into the office of schools in different parts of California I was given the same heavy news: that significant deaths had just occurred that directly affected the classrooms I would be teaching in that day.

You cannot go into a middle or high school on a day like that and pretend that nothing has happened. I don't remember how I coped the first time, but poems did get written. The second time (when two students had committed suicide together), I knew I had to face it directly. So I dashed into the library and found and copied some poems on death. I wrote one of my own using the "surreal juxtaposition" formula I learned from poet-teacher Duane BigEagle. I cut and pasted them all together in a handout.

This lesson was also powerfully appropriate following the attacks on 9/11 while I was the poet-in-residence in an international school in China.

1. After introducing yourself and saying you know about what happened in the school (or in the news), read the poem "Suicide" by Lorca (on worksheet) aloud.
2. Say to the class, "Did the poet really mean someone's 'heart was filling up with broken wings and plastic flowers?' or 'And taking off his gloves, soft ash fell from his hands?' No, not really, but these ideas strongly *convey a feeling*. They are images, and poetic images are the best way to communicate complicated feelings."
3. Ask the class to say some of the issues or questions they are feeling right now. When death, fear, or suicide are mentioned, acknowledge it, saying, "Good, let's see what we can do with that together." Say "Yes, yes" to everything as you write their responses at the top of the board. Be sure that *confused* is included.
4. Ask for words for concrete things (things that are real) that they associate with death and put four or five of them in a list on the left side of the page or the board. They might give you words like *coffin, tears, hospital, blood, gun*. If not, you can begin with two of your own and come back and ask for more.
5. Then ask for words for feelings they associate with loss or death. You might hear *sadness, fear, loneliness*, etc. Be sure *anger* and *lost* are included. Write these in a list on the right hand side of the board or page. Add a couple of your own at the end of each list.
6. Show the students how to make some interesting pairs from the lists to make a strange kind of sense that comes close to what they, or someone else, might be feeling. Try to get them to say some aloud, or do it yourself: "Guilty clock, empty clock, shocked clock, shocked roses, confused furniture, confused roses, guilty roses, guilty coffin, terrified gun, screaming hospital, hallways of hope." Make little remarks about some of these.
7. Ask the class to make their own two lists, a concrete list and a list of associated feelings. Tell them it is all okay; whatever they are thinking or feeling is okay right now. They can write anything they want to; it does not have to be heavy. Then they can use some of the pairs to make a poem.
8. At the end of the class take a few minutes and talk with the students about feelings that might be upsetting. Tell them to think of someone whom they can talk to because it's very important to talk about these things. Have a referral ready for somebody in the school who can listen.

Time and Materials: A class period. A white board or chart paper.

Worksheet

Suicidio
(Quizá fue por no saberte la geometría)
by Federico García Lorca

   El jovencito se olvidaba.
Eran las diez de la mañana.

   Su corazón se iba llenando
de alas rotas y flores de trapo.

   Notó que ya no le quedaba
en la boca más que una palabra.

   Y al quitarse los guantes, caía,
de sus manos, suave ceniza.

   Por el balcón se veía una torre.
El se sintió balcón y torre.

   Vio, sin duda, cómo le miraba
el reloj detenido en su caja.

   Vio su sombra tendida y quieta
en el blanco diván de seda.

   Y el joven rígido, geométrico,
con un hacha rompió el espejo.

   Al romperlo, un gran chorro de sombra
inundó la quimérica alcoba.

Suicide
(Maybe because you flunked geometry)
(Translated by Phyllis Meshulam)

   At ten one morning
the boy forgot.

   His heart was filling up
with broken wings and plastic flowers.

   He noticed that there was
only one word left in his mouth.

   And taking off his gloves, soft ash
fell from his hands.

   From the balcony he could see a tower.
He felt he was both balcony and tower.

   No doubt he saw how the clock
was watching him, stopped in its case.

   He saw his shadow calm and stretched
across the white silk sofa.

   And the boy, stiff, geometrical,
broke the mirror with an axe.

   When he broke it, a fast river of shadow
flooded his room.

Coffin of Grief
  by Karin Faulkner, poet-teacher

Another lost heartbeat
One more loss
A pale grave where time is not ripe.
We are like shocked roses
Watered by guilty tears and hot snow.
What can we add to this coffin of grief?
Confused tears
A clock that runs backward
Angry dirt and sad flowers.

Life
  by Kenyon Zimmer

An ant, too small
to be noticed by many, walked by
as the candle burned, flickering.
I could never be replicated.
Nothing but the earth is my home.
As the stars sing to each other
in the night sky, life makes us endure.
Life Death Loss Love
as the ant slowly slowly passes by.

A Melancholy Gift
  by Rebecca Rosenthal

The guilty tear
A timeless shock
The confused clock
An introverted heart defect
The empty car
My confused hug lowered
Into the amorous pit
Of empty sadness
Tick, tick, gone.

Both student poems are
from Mendocino County.

Advice to Writers
Pair the concrete words and the feelings in ways that you think capture some of what you are experiencing.

Opening the Heart on Paper (Metaphor, Simile) For Grades Four Through Twelve

by Susan Terence (adapted by Phyllis Meshulam)

Imagine: that which is so vital, central, integral—the very life of our being—is so hard to approach in the classroom. We're told to skirt around emotions as powerful as love, abandonment, and loneliness. Poetry bordering on sensuality is taboo in most classrooms as well. So what is the key? How can we go beyond school or societal censorship or even the reluctance that young adults themselves have in exposing their inner emotions?

We use art. We use literature. We use music. I cheat. I bring my poetry lessons centering on love or lost love to classrooms a few weeks prior to Valentine's Day. I know it's fraudulent, but it's a hook. Students don't resist. (They've all been acculturated with the unspoken obligation to express love and gratitude to their loved ones in mid-February.) To counter the commercial aspects, I don't bring in saccharine greeting card poems. Instead, I bring translations from the ninth-, tenth-, and eleventh-century Japanese court poetry by Ono No Komachi and Lady Horikawa, or love poems by Pablo Neruda, Donald Hall, and Kenneth Patchen.

1. Mention that the Japanese poems were written by women a thousand years ago or more. These poets lived at court and, because of the strong emphasis on the arts at that time and place, had an opportunity to achieve distinction as writers that has taken a very long time for other women around the world to catch up to. This is a good opportunity for a discussion of the status of women, now, then, and in-between.

2. Read together the Ono No Komachi poem. Ask students if the feeling expressed—powerlessness in a relationship—is exclusive to women in ninth-century Japan, or if men and women still experience that.

3. For younger students' lessons, I present poems in which students have created metaphors for a broken heart, happy heart, angry heart. ("My heart, like a car without gas / My heart, like an empty house . . .")

4. One of the biggest surprises in teaching this lesson came when I worked with a group of male teenagers in Hugh Stickney's woodshop class at John O'Connell Technical High School. The students questioned their teacher about Donald Hall's line, "Never before has inside spoken to inside." He spoke to them candidly about the differences between being "in lust" and being "in love." One seventeen-year-old asked, "But how do you know when you've found someone you can speak inside to inside?" Poetry can help answer that question.

5. Students also enjoy using rubber stamps to embellish their love and out-of-love poems to create poetic "Valentines." It is awe-inspiring to see adolescent joy and fragility caught on paper.

Materials: The worksheet. Optional poems to include are "Questions" by Donald Hall, "What There Is" by Kenneth Patchen, "Colors" by Yevgeny Yevthusehnko, "You Have What I Look For" by Jaime Sabines, number XVI from *20 Love Poems and a Song of Despair* by Pablo Neruda, and "How long will it last" by Lady Horikawa. Optional: rubber stamps for decorating.

Worksheet

The seaweed gatherer's weary feet
by Ono No Komachi

The seaweed gatherer's weary feet
keep coming back to my shore.
Doesn't he know
there's no harvest for him
in this uncaring bay?

(Translated by Jane Hirshfield)

My Heart
by Glenn Garcia, S.F. County

My heart loves you
as much as the woman who gave birth to it.
Every time I get close to you
my heart beats 140 times,
two times its normal rate.

My heart is like a magnet.
It wants to be with you
every time I think of you
in the morning
in the afternoon
and especially at night . . .

Nothing Else
by Cody Johnson, S.F. County

My heart,
like an eagle of bright red
soaring through the warm
spring air like there's nothing
else in the world but a true
love.

My Great Heart
by Robert Marquez, S.F. County

My heart like an air bubble getting
popped . . . My heart like a melting
ice cream on a Sunday morning . . .
My heart like the beginning of a school semester—
My heart
my great heart . . .

Waiting
by Luis Villaseñor, S.F. County

My heart, like a poor man's wallet,
is empty
like a child at an orphanage waiting
to be loved . . .

Too Late
by Laqueta Crach, S.F. County

My heart is a fat red "F"
on your history report.
It's totally ashamed of itself.
It gave you no credit,
no matter how hard you've tried.
It knows you'd work hard
all through the night.
Now it's too late.
You have no more self-esteem.
And there are no more history reports
for the fat red letter to see.

Like a Bird
by Kevin Fitch, S.F. County

My heart
is like a
bird with no wings
falling out
of the air

Still Waiting
by Luis Leiva, S.F. County

Your heart, like an empty penny jar
still waiting to be filled with love . . .

Advice to Writers
Make metaphors and similes for your heart.

California Poets In The Schools

The Anti-Ode
For Grades Four Through Twelve

by Blake More

The ode is a poem that praises or celebrates a subject. It has a venerable history, going back to Pindar in ancient Greece and Horace in early Rome. Some of Pindar's odes were set to music for choral dances, while Horace's have inspired many ode writers since his time. Odes were also popular with the English Romantic poets. Among the more famous odes from the period are "Ode to a Nightingale" and "Ode on a Grecian Urn" by John Keats; "Dejection: An Ode" by Samuel Taylor Coleridge; and "Ode to the West Wind" and "To a Skylark" by Percy Bysshe Shelley. Most traditional odes are written in exalted language and meant to glorify and bring dignity to their subject matter.

Much later, one of the more prolific writers of odes, Chilean poet Pablo Neruda, found joy in praising the ordinary, such as socks, watermelon, and olive oil. The anti-ode degrades the ode one step further—into the realm of the humorous and/or profane. An anti-ode can make a social statement—against TV, deforestation, war—or be about something more personal, such as poison oak or a broken arm. The idea is to use the ode form to poetically rail against a peeve that is so close to your heart that it gives you hives.

1. Give a brief age-appropriate history of odes based on the above introduction.

2. Do a group brainstorm to list a few everyday common things that drive us crazy, or that are loathsome. Make sure this poem is about things/objects—not people. Write them on the board as the students state their pet peeves.

3. Pick one of these "common things" and write an anti-ode to it as a class. Act as the scribe to create the anti-ode on the board.

4. Read aloud my sample anti-ode on the worksheet. Read it with feeling!

5. Tell the students that they will now write their own anti-odes, and give them the following instructions:
   - The trick to anti-odes is to observe the thing you are anti-praising in extreme detail, as an observational scientist would.
   - Use the five senses in your ode (smells like, tastes like, feels like, looks like, sounds like).
   - Make comparisons (similes and metaphors): TV is a dirty rat, chocolate is mud on my shoes.
   - Set a mood—angry, funny, resigned, jealous, and so on—or pick more than one.
   - Personify: Write the poem to your object of loathing as if it were a person.
   - Write a couple of starter lines on the board. "_____! You . . ." (object of loathing such as "television!" or "name tag") or "You _____, how I hate you . . ."

6. Give students plenty of time to write.

7. Leave time at the end for students to read their anti-odes, and cheer loudly for their poems!

Worksheet

Anti-Ode to a Nametag
by Blake More, poet-teacher

Oh how I hate you nametag
from the very start
back when I first encountered you
sometime in kindergarten
too young to write my name on you
(someone else had to do it for me)
a strange and loathsome social obstacle course
you were garbage then
now you are much more
a degrading ozone
masked as a trite costume
your overflowing landfill self
drawing eyeballs to my chest
"oh helloooooo . . . Blake"
as if I didn't notice how these fake people
miraculously knew my name
before discerning my hair color or slant of my nose
before noticing I was a complete stranger
oh disdainful nametag
you smell like people trying too hard
to get to know each other
in your sham attempts to be easy and polite
you are no better than bad air
the drone of a stale air conditioner
competing with a fuzzy p.a.
the conference speech blather making me yawn
as I listen to the nimrods who gave you to me
my name so perfectly printed
with a silly title underneath
who insisted that I wear your meaningless nothingness
I loath you as your instigators yammer on and on
on and on and on
and it takes every jigger-full of restraint
for me not to jump up and tear you from my breast
you cancer of societal norms
yet I don't, but instead dream
of the moment I can tear you off
throw you in the dumpster
where you belong

Seven Divided by 100 Equals Too Many Books
by Jasper Bayless, Mendocino County

Oh books
you look so overwhelming sometimes
there's just too many of you
you smell like fallen trees
you feel too smooth
like all the factories making covers
and polluting the air
you taste like sour tarts
that have been breathed on
by morning breath
you sound like ear-popping thunder
why are there so many of you
can I ever read you all?

Prompts
Other student poets have written about a wet towel, a kazoo, school, soy sauce, cigarettes, glare, bad rap songs, a chair, rain, homework.

Emotions: First-Time Experience, Loss of Innocence For Grades Ten Through Twelve

by Shelley Savren

In poetry, we don't want to state our feelings, but to describe what happened to make us feel a certain way. We don't want to tell our readers what to feel. We want them to feel it. One of the most important parts of writing poems is using our imagination. We use it in restaurants when ordering food, when doing science experiments, when inventing something—and especially when empathizing with someone who's hurting.

Poems also use the five senses, express feelings, and create images. Today, many poems are written in free verse, use an economy of words, and are concerned with the line. A poet can create natural breath lines by reading the poem aloud and starting a new line every time she or he takes a breath.

And poems have a kinship to music. They both have rhythm; they create patterns or emphasize sounds. In one of the sample poems for this lesson, Bruce Weigl uses alliteration, repeating consonants to create a pattern of sounds when he writes: "My wife wakes me" and "Shake the lies loose from his lips." In her poem, Mabel Robles creates patterns with "thrilling . . . / tempting . . ." and repeats syntax in: "a fire begins to burn . . . / the raven steals a kiss. / A trace of innocence . . . lost."

1. "For this lesson, we want to focus on emotions in poems. It's important to describe an activity or event that made us feel a certain way. A good poem will elicit an emotional response from the reader as well."

2. "As we grow up, we experience things that change us and make us face the truth. We lose our innocence and learn something about life that we didn't realize before. We become responsible and cannot go back to being a child anymore because we know too much. Examples can include our first experience with death, our first time driving, or a first kiss."

3. Read the poem by Bruce Weigl. Ask the students what happened to the boy in the poem. What did he feel, and how did the experience in the poem change him? How did he lose his innocence?

4. Then discuss how the poet does not tell the reader what the boy was feeling, but describes it. How does he do that? Ask the students what lines stood out for them. Point out lines like, "His man's muscled shoulders / Shake with the weight of what he can't set right no matter what / But one last time he tries to stay a child" and "If I let go he'll fly to pieces before me." This last one also likens the boy to the bird he shot.

5. Ask a student to read the poem by Mabel Robles and ask the class what the speaker was feeling and how she lost her innocence, pointing out the last three lines.

6. Let the students write poems describing a first-time experience where they lost their innocence. Use the advice to writers on the worksheet for instructions.

7. Finally, students read their poems out loud. After each student reads, one person responds with a detail he or she liked. All responses must be positive, since these are drafts, and this is not a time to critique, but a time to acknowledge and validate.

Worksheet

Snowy Egret
by Bruce Weigl

My neighbor's boy has lifted his father's shotgun and stolen
Down to the backwaters of the Elizabeth
And in the moon he's blasted a snowy egret
From the shallows it stalked for small fish.

Midnight. My wife wakes me. He's in the backyard
With a shovel so I go down half-drunk with pills
That let me sleep to see what I can see and if it's safe.
The boy doesn't hear me come across the dewy grass.
He says through tears he has to bury it,
He says his father will kill him
And he digs until the hole is deep enough and gathers
The egret carefully into his arms
As if not to harm the blood-splattered wings
Gleaming in the flashlight beam.

His man's muscled shoulders
Shake with the weight of what he can't set right no matter what,
But one last time he tries to stay a child, sobbing
Please don't tell . . .
He says he only meant to flush it from the shadows,
He only meant to watch it fly
But the shot spread too far
Ripping into the white wings
Spanned awkwardly for a moment
Until it glided into brackish death.

I want to grab his shoulders,
Shake the lies loose from his lips but he hurts enough,
He burns with shame for what he's done,
With fear for his hard father's
fists I've seen crash down on him for so much less.
I don't know what to do but hold him.
If I let go he'll fly to pieces before me.
What a time we share, that can make a good boy steal away,
Wiping out from the blue face of the pond
What he hadn't even known he loved, blasting
Such beauty into nothing.

First Kiss
by Mabel Robles, Ventura County

The cold, dark night
releases its malignant
pure evil . . .
an essence
that brings pleasure
to a lonely heart.

There is movement all
       around
from those ready
to devour the lamb . . .
prepare the sacrifice.
They dance to the music
intense . . .
thrilling . . .
tempting . . .

Two sweaty bodies nearly
       touch.
They dance
absorbing the heat
of the moment.

Luminescent
changing colored lights
ricochet off savages
or rather those
consciously unaware
of the passion
which fills the air.

Her arms
on his shoulders,
his dark brown eyes
on her face.

The music drums its beat . . .
a fire begins to burn . . .
the raven steals a kiss.
A trace of innocence . . .
       lost.

Advice for Writers
Write a poem describing a first-time experience and loss of innocence. Think of an experience that changed you profoundly, where you learned something new and can never go back to the way you were—for example, your first encounter with death. You know too much; you are no longer innocent. Remember to describe, not state, your feelings, and look for opportunities to create rhythm.

Detailed Memories: Emotions Triggered by an Object or Event For Grades Ten Through Twelve

by Shelley Savren

Details help us understand what's going on in a poem. The more specific the detail, the easier it is to imagine the picture; the more abstract, the less interesting. If readers are to enter a poem, they need to know where to sit down. We need rich descriptions and images so we can imagine the scene or the feeling. If we zoom in on an object or event that triggered those details, emotion will burst through in the poem.

As in the "First Time" lesson [see page 110], discuss the elements that comprise poetry. All poems come from our imagination. Poems are musical, sensual, and they tell about something, as stories do, but they do that in a rhythmical form, paying attention to the line.

Poems use a concise language. Each word must be exact and important to the poem. Also, most poetry today is written in free verse without rhyme. The father of free verse, Walt Whitman, saw everyone and every little thing as important. In his poem, "Song of Myself," he wrote, "I believe a leaf of grass is no less than the journey-work of the stars." He zeroed in on the smallest details: "And brown ants in the little wells."

1. "Today, we're going to focus on details. Imagine that you're in an art museum looking at a portrait of a woman wearing a royal blue dress. When you come closer to the portrait, you see that there are stripes of black on the dress. When you step back again, you realize that that's what makes the wrinkles."

2. "Today, we're going to put 'wrinkles' into our poems. Doing that makes the picture described in the poem look more real. We have to get in close to notice details, and sometimes we just need to pay attention. And we can use our imagination to see things that could be inside an object, or we can see that object through a new lens. Whitman saw the grass as many things, including 'the beautiful uncut hair of graves.'"

3. "Often we associate certain objects with experiences we've had. Today, we're going to zoom into an object or event, see all the details, and allow them to trigger a memory or emotion."

4. Read the poem by David St. John and talk about how the small boy watched his grandma leave on a train. He was holding an iris; as he got older he could look into an iris and remember that train taking his grandmother away. The emotion comes through in the details: "A train inside this iris. / It's a child's finger bearded in black banners," and "& now believe me: The train / Is gone. The old woman is dead, & the boy. The iris curls."

5. Ask a student to read the poem by Cameron Brooks, where a boy remembers that the last time he saw his father, his father picked him up and promised to return, but didn't. Point out that emotion comes through in the details: "I watched him vanish that night, / eight years to this day."

6. Ask students to write poems describing an object or event in great detail, allowing a memory related to it to trigger an emotion. Use the advice to writers on the worksheet.

7. Lastly, let students read their poems out loud (with no apologies). After each student reads, another student and the teacher should comment positively on what they liked about the poem.

Worksheet

Iris
(Vivian St. John 1881–1974)
  by David St. John

There is a train inside this iris:

You think I'm crazy, & like to say boyish
& outrageous things. No, there is

A train inside this iris.

It's a child's finger bearded in black banners.
A single window like a child's nail,

A darkened porthole lit by the white, angular face

Of an old woman, or perhaps the boy beside her in the stuffy,
Hot compartment. Her hair is silver, & sweeps

Back off her forehead, onto her cold and bruised shoulders.

The prairies fail along Chicago. Past the five
Lakes. Into the black woods of her New York; & as I bend

Close above the iris, I see the train

Drive deep into the damp heart of its stem, & the gravel
Of the garden path

Cracks under my feet as I walk this long corridor

Of elms, arched
Like the ceiling of a French railway pier where a boy

With pale curls holding

A fresh iris is waving goodbye to a grandmother, gazing
A long time

Into the flower, as if he were looking some great

Distance, or down an empty garden path & he believes a man
Is walking toward him, working

Dull shears in one hand; & now believe me: The train

Is gone. The old woman is dead, & the boy. The iris curls,
On its stalk, in the shade

Of those elms: Where something like the icy & bitter fragrance

In the wake of a woman who's just swept past you on her way
Home   & you remain.

Father
  by Cameron Brooks, Ventura County

Ducking through the door,
striding across the room,
        he came.
His square face set with a smile,
        his eyes round and dark,
        sparkling in the light.
Five steps and he was across
    my room.
        There I was standing,
        a smile on my face.
        There I was standing,
looking straight up for miles
        just to see his face.
His massive hand came down,
        lightly patting me on the head.
Using both hands,
        he effortlessly lifted me into
            the air.
        From way up there,
I saw my home in a whole new way.
I laughed, I giggled . . . I was happy.
He said he couldn't stay long,
        but that was all right.
I knew he would be back,
        and that's all that mattered.
He placed me on the floor
        and said good-bye.
I watched him vanish that night,
        eight years to this day.

Advice to Writers
Write a poem about someone you loved or cared about who left you, or create an image of someone who's gone and whom you miss. Describe what happened in extreme detail, as if you are putting that person under a microscope for the reader to study. Create a picture with so much emotion folded in that it hurts to look at it.

The Power of Negative Space For High School Students
by Prartho Sereno

I am a poet who also paints. And as a painter, I am always captivated by the power of negative space: the way a subject can be evoked by carefully rendering the area around it. When we attend to details *outside* the subject, our perspective is reversed and the subject takes on surprising nuance and depth. This approach also works with words. Describing what is *not* there or isn't true seems to evoke, almost by magic, what *is*. And for high school students, starting with the negative could well be the most natural way of falling into a poem!

1. Start with a discussion of the negative in visual art. You will want some copies of paintings that rely heavily on negative space for their effect. In my experience, watercolor is the best medium for this. Search the Internet for *negative space watercolor painting*. Linda Kemp is a contemporary painter whose work often uses negative space.
2. Now you can try it with words: Using the following list of negative prompts, go around the room, asking students to complete a phrase aloud. This step is best when the pressure is low, the atmosphere playful—a kind of warm-up, process-not-product event.
   Prompts:
   It's not that . . . I'm not saying . . . I don't care about . . . I'm not . . . I don't know . . . There are no . . . It was never . . . She/He never . . . I/We/They didn't want . . . I didn't see . . . You couldn't hear . . . I don't remember . . . That year, we didn't . . .
3. Alternatively, you can create a group poem on the board, varying the prompts as your poetic intuition dictates. This way, the students can volunteer lines as they're inspired. Group poems are great warm-ups, and often enough a lively poem finds its way through the collective voice.
4. Ask for a student volunteer to read the sample poem, "Talc," by Jane Hirshfield. Before the reader begins, instruct the students that, as active listeners, their job is to find at least one segment/line/image/moment they like. This not only engages each student with the poem, but it bypasses cerebral quibbles over "meaning." What we like (or has touched us) brings us more naturally to the "heart" of the poem, where we can begin to explore *how* it moves us as readers.
5. Let the lines and images that speak to students guide the discussion, but eventually bring it back to the power of the negative. Note also the paradox: Everything invisible to the speaker in "Talc" does, in fact, have a vivid presence in the poem. The things that the speaker "scarcely saw" are palpable to us, the reader. How does this contribute to the poem's effect? Also read "Poem."
6. Give the students the list of negative prompts in #2. They may want to use the prompts to explore a potent memory, as in the sample poem, "Talc." Or they may simply let the prompts lead the way. Creating their own negative-space prompt is also fine.
7. If someone gets stuck, I tell him or her to pick up the old prompt, or even a new one, and go on. Often students think a new thought won't be logically connected to their poem, but actually, such a poetic leap often gives their line of thought a needed lift—out of the over-wrought explanations of the left brain into the spacious unpredictability of the right.
8. Use the last ten minutes for courageous students to read their work aloud—and for applause!

Time and Materials: I recommend an hour to allow for sharing. You will need printed or projected images of negative-space paintings, a way to share the prompts (on the back of the worksheet, on chart paper, or projected), and the worksheet with the sample poems.

Worksheet

Talc

by Jane Hirshfield

When you phoned I was far, and sleeping,
but they brought me the message and I ran,
I ran to the phone where you were,
you were speaking, we two were speaking,
when I ran back to the room I no longer
knew we would speak again. Twenty minutes
and I was gone, there was a plane,
and another, there was a friend who took
me to you, you were asleep. I didn't know
there was still any question, I only learned
later, everything later, weeks later I was
still frightened of all that I learned.
I swear though I knew it was there I scarcely
saw the hose taped to your mouth, its ridges
that breathed in case you did not; scarcely saw
the twin tubes coming out of your chest or
the blood running through them and into the pump
that returned to your wrist, quietly, steadily,
what belonged there. The slenderer tubes
that entered the side of your neck I scarcely
noticed; not the empty ones waiting for something
not needed, not the ones drawing fluids
from three labeled bags. They had washed you,
I barely noticed the yellow stains and the blood
that remained on your skin. They had cut you,
I did not see the bandages holding the length
of the chest, they lay where I should have been
lying, I did not understand. I did not see
the wounds on your side where some scalpel or saw
had been dropped or some heated or iced tool
had burned. The monitor's chiming was nothing,
someone would come, they would turn it off.
The slash stapling the crease of your thigh was
nothing. When the nurse turned the white valve
near the collarbones' nest before opening one
on the wrist, there was not one cell of my body
that needed to understand. I barely felt the bars
where my hand fitted into your hand, the rail
that days afterward still tracked my cheek.
The urine that drained to the sack below us must
have been warm, I must have touched it, I should
have known it was warm with your warmth but I did not.
I waited. I knew that the sweetness I smelled
on your body was powder, was baby powder, I did
not understand, but I knew they had given you back
to this world for a second time and I waited
for you to agree. I waited for you to open your eyes,
a first time, another, another. I waited until
you were sure, until every part of you stayed.

Poem

by Tashira Miggins, Marin County

I'm not trying to say
horses aren't a miracle
I'm not trying to say
whales don't lie
I'm not trying to say
love leads to loneliness
I'm not trying to say
almonds are orange
I'm not trying to say
girls are luckier than boys
I'm not trying to say
ghosts can keep secrets
And I'm sure not trying to say
poetry is easy
Because it's not.

Dear Poetic Nay-Sayers,

Fill your poem with details of every kind: smells and sounds, colors and movement, touch. Let us know as much as you can about everything outside your subject (and if you don't know exactly what your subject is, so much the better—you can discover it along with your reader).

Acknowledgments

Heart's core gratitude to: all poets and publishers who donated rights; the CPitS board, which believed in the project and that I could guide it without "handholding"; Karen Lewis, board secretary, who nevertheless provided quite a bit of handholding in the form of advice and attagirls; Tina Pasquinzo, CPitS Director of Operations, for near-constant availability and constant good spirits; the Co Eds, my assistant editors Cathy Barber and Seretta Martin, who, even when we realized what a tiger we had by the tail, still kept hanging on with me; field editors Tresha Faye Hacfner for fresh perspectives and Richard Newsham for going way above and beyond; designer Blake More, for pacifying the tiger while enhancing its beauty; Carolyn Miller and Fernando Castro for copy editing and gifts of time and acuity; Mark Oatney, Mendocino art teacher, for inspiring student artwork; all the teachers who have welcomed us into their classrooms and given us a chance to "road-test" these lessons, and in particular, the teachers with whom I have worked this year from whose nurturing and stimulating environments poems, pictures, and videos arose: Diane Beckmann, Carly Costello, Mariya Cree, Susan Foshay, Gary Griffith, Suzanne Heiser, Ellie Katzel, Juanita Miller, Peggy McClure, Sal Pagano, Rhonda Pipkin, Amber Stiving, Crystal Tsutsui, Gwen Watson, and Nikki Winovich; Jerry Meshulam, for nonstop encouragement, and for copiously sharing his videography and Photoshop skills; the poet-teachers who spread the good news of poetry by generously sharing their lessons in this book and by teaching them in classrooms throughout California; the trees that gave their lives to make the leaves of this book; the children whose pictures and poems show that so much is possible.

And more gratitude from the heart's deep core to the following benefactors who made vision reality: Flock of Muses: California Arts Council and National Endowment for the Arts; Clio, Muse of Epic Poetry: Albert Flynn DeSilver; Muses: Warren Arnold, Margaret Caminsky-Shapiro, Daryl and Phyllis Chinn, Pat Ferris, Diana Griggs, Christine Heaney, Jerry Meshulam, Richard Newsham, Ted Sexauer.

—Phyllis Meshulam

Credits

"La Misión/The Mission" from *Body in Flames/Cuerpo en Llamas* by Francisco X. Alarcón (Chronicle Books, 1990). Copyright © Francisco X. Alarcón. Used by permission of Francisco X. Alarcón.

"The Turtle" by anonymous prehistoric artist. Reprinted from *A Chant a Mile Long: California Poets in the Schools Statewide Anthology 1990.*

"Lost Dog" from *The Human Line*. Copyright © 2007 by Ellen Bass. Reprinted with the permission of the Permissions Company, Inc., on behalf of Copper Canyon Press, www.coppercanyonpress.org.

"Pasajera/In Passing" from *A Cage of Transparent Words* (2007) by Alberto Blanco. Translated by Judith Infante. Used by permission of Bitter Oleander Press and Alberto Blanco.

"Father" by Cameron Brooks. Reprinted from *Listen to the Wild: California Poets in the Schools Statewide Anthology 1996.*

"Hearts" by Buena Vista Alternative School Students, San Francisco. Reprinted from *Heart Flip: California Poets in the Schools Statewide Anthology 2001.*

"Wild as the Wind" by Flora Chen. Reprinted from *Parting the Future: California Poets in the Schools Statewide Anthology 2011.*

"Too Late" by Laqueta Crach. Reprinted from *Wilderness of Dreams: California Poets in the Schools Statewide Anthology 1998.*

"Moon and Observer" by Mark Deamer. Reprinted from *Moon Won't Leave Me Alone, California Poets in the Schools Statewide Anthology 2003 – 2004.*

"Forest Branches and Notes" by Sara de Torres. Reprinted from *Sing to the Heart of the Forest: California Poets in the Schools Statewide Anthology 2013.*

"Looking at the Night Sky" by Daniel Doan. Reprinted from *Parting the Future: California Poets in the Schools Statewide Anthology 2011.*

"Black" by Tony Dorin. Reprinted from *Turning into Stars: California Poets in the Schools Statewide Anthology 2012.*

"Planaria" by Chris Dunnibier. Reprinted from *Forgotten Languages: California Poets in the Schools Statewide Anthology 1985.*

"A lake. A night without a moon" and "There are waterfalls" from *Lost Body* by Terry Ehret. Copyright © 1992 by Terry Ehret. Reprinted with the permission of Terry Ehret and the Permissions Company, Inc., on behalf of Copper Canyon Press, www.coppercanyonpress.org.

"Mi Mano" by Aldo Encizo. Translated as "My Hand" by Jim Cartwright. Reprinted from *My Song Is the Light: California Poets in the Schools Statewide Anthology 2007.*

"Hand pictures" by Molly Fisk and Anne Woodward. Reprinted from *Belonging to California: California Poets in the Schools Statewide Anthology 1997*.

"Untitled" from *on the wing* by Douglas Florian, copyright © 1996 by Douglas Florian. Used with permission of Douglas Florian.

Hieroglyphs which accompany "A lake. A night without a moon" and "There are waterfalls" by John L. Foster. Reprinted from *Lost Body* by Terry Ehret with the permission of the Permissions Company, Inc., on behalf of Copper Canyon Press, www.coppercanyonpress.org.

"My Heart" by Glenn Garcia. Reprinted from *Wilderness of Dreams: California Poets in the Schools Statewide Anthology 1998*.

"My Heart" by Devon Garlick. Reprinted from *Parting the Future: California Poets in the Schools Statewide Anthology 2011*.

"Big Brown Eyes" by Sage Gautier. Reprinted from *Border Voices Anthology 2010*.

"Mountain Awakening" by Jenny Gealy. Reprinted from *Wood, Water, Air and Fire: The Anthology of Mendocino Women Poets*, Potshard Press, 1998. Used by permission of the Gealy family.

"Silver" by Greyson Gove. Reprinted from *My Song Is the Light: California Poets in the Schools Statewide Anthology 2007*.

"The Song of Amergin" from *Gods and Fighting Men* (1904). Translated by Lady Augusta Gregory.

"Ode to the Amoeba" by Arthur Guiterman. Reprinted with permission of Richard Sclove.

"When I Move to the Mountains" by Tresha Haefner. Reprinted from *Amarillo Bay* (2011).

"Gateways of Hope" by Cherith Hasegawa. Reprinted from *On the Other Side of Tomorrow: California Poets in the Schools Statewide Anthology 2008*.

"Jatun Sacha" from *Sun Under Wood* by Robert Hass (Ecco Press, 1996), copyright © by Robert Hass. Used with permission of Robert Hass.

"Let us gather in a flourishing way" from *Rebozos of Love We Have Woven Sudor de Pueblos on Our Back* by Juan Felipe Herrera (Toltecas and Aztlan Publications, 1974). Used with permission of Juan Felipe Herrera.

"Girl Sleuth" from *Practical Water* by Brenda Hillman (Wesleyan University Press, 2009). Copyright © by Brenda Hillman. Used with permission of Brenda Hillman.

"The seaweed gatherer's weary feet" from *The Ink Dark Moon: Love Poems* by Ono No Komachi and Izumi Shikibu, *Women of the Ancient Japanese Court* (NY: Vintage Classics, 1990). Co-translated by Jane Hirshfield with Mariko Aratami; translation © 1988 by Jane Hirshfield. Used by permission of Jane Hirshfield.

"Talc" from *The Lives of the Heart* by Jane Hirshfield (HarperCollins, 1997). Copyright© by Jane Hirshfield. Used by permission of Jane Hirshfield.

"It's a Blue Meteor Falling" by Alex Intara. Reprinted from *Parting the Future: California Poets in the Schools Statewide Anthology 2011*.

"Pied Beauty" from *Poems of Gerard Manley Hopkins* (1918), by Gerard Manley Hopkins.

"Untitled," by José Silva Huey. Reprinted from *Moon Won't Leave Me Alone: California Poets in the Schools Statewide Anthology 2003-2004*.

"Nothing Else" by Cody Johnson. Reprinted from *Wilderness of Dreams: California Poets in the Schools Statewide Anthology 1998*.

"Walking Beside a Creek" and "In an Old Apple Orchard" from *Flying at Night: Poems 1965–1985* by Ted Kooser. Copyright © 2005 by Ted Kooser. Reprinted by permission of the University of Pittsburgh Press.

"On the Other Side of the Poem," from *Fun yener zayt lid/On the Other Side of the Poem* by Rachel H. Korn (Y.L. Peretz Farlag, 1962). English translation from the Yiddish by Seymour Levitan, copyright © 1986 by Seymour Levitan. Used with permission of Seymour Levitan and the Korn estate.

"The World of Me!" by Erica Larson. Reprinted from *My Song Is the Light: California Poets in the Schools Statewide Anthology 2007*.

"The Emigrant" by Brian Lee. Reprinted from *A Tree in the Sky: California Poets in the Schools Statewide Anthology 1995*.

"Waiting" by Luis Leiva. Reprinted from *Wilderness of Dreams: California Poets in the Schools Statewide Anthology 1998*.

"Angel Island Poem 12," by an anonymous Chinese detainee. From *Island* (University of Washington Press, 1980, 2014). Translated by Genny Lim. Translation copyright © by Genny Lim and Judy Yung, 1980. Used by permission of Genny Lim and Judy Yung.

"The Moon's the North Wind's Cooky" from *The Congo and Other Poems* (1915) by Vachel Lindsay.

"Romance Sonámbulo" from *Primero Romancero Gitano* (1930) by Federico García Lorca. Used by permission of Fundación Federico García Lorca.

"Suicidio" from *Canciones* (1926) by Federico García Lorca. Used by permission of Fundación Federico García Lorca.

"The Woman Who Lives on Wall Street" by Dylan Love. Reprinted from *Border Voices Anthology 2013*.

"My Great Heart" by Robert Marquez. Reprinted from *Wilderness of Dreams: California Poets in the Schools Statewide Anthology 1998*.

"My Road Back Home" by Vincent "Burtsie" Maruffo. Reprinted from *Moon Won't Leave Me Alone: California Poets in the Schools Statewide Anthology 2003–04*.

"The Silver Eclipse" by David Melendez-Perdomo. Reprinted from *Border Voices Anthology 2010*.

"Poem" by Tashira Miggins. Reprinted from *100 Parades: California Poets in the Schools Statewide Anthology 2000*.

"W" by Laurel Moeslein. Reprinted from *Wilderness of Dreams: California Poets in the Schools Statewide Anthology 1998*.

"Small Heart" by Maisie Moore. Reprinted from *Turning into Stars: California Poets in the Schools Statewide Anthology 2012*.

"Dream Colors" by Nayeli Orozco. Reprinted from *The Moon of Many Things Mendocino County Anthology 2013*.

"Creek Sestina" by Dane Paulson, Tessla Carlson, Sam Fanucchi, Ana Cruz, and Anna Cline. Reprinted from *Turning into Stars: California Poets in the Schools Anthology 2012*.

"Shelf City" by Nathaniel Pick. Reprinted from *Border Voices Anthology 2007*.

"My Hands Are Everything" by Lauren Raith. Reprinted from *My Song Is the Light: California Poets in the Schools Statewide Anthology 2007*.

"First Kiss" by Mabel Robles. Reprinted from *Belonging to California: California Poets in the Schools Statewide Anthology 1997*.

"Oh, Boom of You, Basketball, You Make Life" by Ava Rognlien. Reprinted from *Parting the Future: California Poets in the Schools Statewide Anthology 2011*.

"Iris," copyright © 1994, 2014 by David St. John. Used by permission of the author.

"Fog" from *Chicago Poems* (1916) by Carl Sandburg.

"Ozymandias" by Percy Bysshe Shelley, from *The Examiner,* January 1918.

"Susan's Muses" by Susan Sibbet. Reprinted from *What the World Hears: California Poets in the Schools Statewide Anthology 2009*.

"How Poetry Comes to Me" from *No Nature* by Gary Snyder (Pantheon, 1992). Copyright © by Gary Snyder. Used with permission of Gary Snyder.

"Magpie's Song" from *Turtle Island* (New Directions, 1974). Copyright © by Gary Snyder. Used with permission of Gary Snyder.

"Raven's Beak River at the End" from *Mountains and Rivers Without End* by Gary Snyder (Counterpoint, 1996). Copyright © by Gary Snyder. Used with permission of Gary Snyder.

"Tomorrow" by Sarah Stretch. Reprinted from *On the Other Side of Tomorrow: California Poets in the Schools Statewide Anthology 2008*.

"The Stadium at Midnight" by Jocelyn Tran. Reprinted from *Parting the Future: California Poets in the Schools Statewide Anthology 2011*.

"The Strange Weather" by Alice Truong. Reprinted from *A Tree in the Sky: California Poets in the Schools Statewide Anthology 1995*.

"Casey at the Bat" by Ernest Lawrence Thayer, first published in 1888 by the *San Francisco Examiner*.

"It's Magic!" by Raymond Vallee. Reprinted from *Parting the Future: California Poets in the Schools Statewide Anthology 2011*.

"Waiting" by Luis Villaseñor. Reprinted from *Wilderness of Dreams: California Poets in the Schools Statewide Anthology 1998*.

"Snowy Egret" (1988), copyright © by Bruce Weigl. Used with permission of Bruce Weigl.

"Ode to a Volvox" by David Weiskoph. Reprinted from *Forgotten Languages: California Poets in the Schools Statewide Anthology 1985*.

"Fragments of Sappho" from *Sappho: Memoir, Text, Selected Renderings and a Literal Translation,* translated by Henry Thornton Wharton (Brentano's, 1920 and 1887).

"Untitled" from *Many Winters* by Nancy C. Wood. Courtesy of Nancy Wood Literary Trust. Copyright © 1974 by Nancy C. Wood.

"Mondo Bongo" from *The Sound of Dreams Remembered* (Loveletter Editions, 2006). Copyright© 2001 and 2006 by Al Young. Reprinted with permission of Al Young.

Illustrations

Chilion, by **Emma Jones**, Mendocino County...11
Paintbrush, by **Diana Valle**, Sonoma County...15, 81
Hands, by **Molly Fisk and Anne Woodward**...17
Puddle, by **Diana Valle**, Sonoma County..19
Dancing Spoon, by **Diana Valle**, Sonoma County..21
Tree, by **Brittany Madden**, Mendocino County..23, 31, 37
Moon and Observer, by **Mark Deamer**...25, 43
Drum, by **José Morfín**, Sonoma County...27
Spiderman, by **Sergio Villagomez**, Sonoma County 29
Bamboo, by **Kate Wollman**, Mendocino County..35
Bat and Ball, by **Sergio Villagomez**, Sonoma County...39
Sphinx, by **Alexia Sanchez**, Sonoma County..41
Hummingbird, by **Diana Valle**, Sonoma County..45
On the Other Side of, by **Cherith Osegawa**, Ventura County......................................47
Turtle, by anonymous prehistoric artist..49
Hieroglyphs, by **Edgar Cazares Carreno**, Sonoma County..53
Hieroglyphs accompanying prose poems, by **John L. Foster**.....................................53
Deer, by **Edson Guillen**, Sonoma County..55
Calligraphy, by **Hideko Oga**..55
Turkey, by **Sakota Calvino**, Mendocino County..59
Hearts, by students from **Buena Vista Alternative School**, San Francisco and **Kyra Harr**, Mendocino.........63, 107
Snowflake, by **Diana Valle**, Sonoma County...65
Raven, by **Tommy Ran**, Sonoma County...67
Lyre, by **Diana Valle**, Sonoma County...69
Muse, by **José Morfín**, Sonoma County..71
Musical Notes, by **Sara de Torres**, San Diego County...73
Hearts, by **Joslynn Georganas**, Mendocino County..75
Self-portrait, by **Diana Valle**, Sonoma County 77
Corn, by **Aimee Gordon**, Mendocino County 79
Tree with bird, by **Sara de Torres**, San Diego County 83
Cow, by **G. Charlie Hernandez**, Sonoma County 85
Chinese characters, by **Hideko Oga** 89
Amoeba, by **Alma Salyer**, Mendocino County 93
Bird & Bush, by **Kaylin Harr**, Mendocino County 97
Bird, by **Beyulah Anderson**, Mendocino County 99
Parachute, by **Cole Kossivas**, Mendocino County...101
Hello, My Name Is, by **Jazmine Atherton-Walsh**, Mendocino County 109
Horse, by **Prartho Sereno**..115

Recommended Resources for Teachers

Alarcón, Francisco X. *Angels Ride Bikes: And Other Fall Poems.* New York: Lee & Low Books, 1999. Illustrated bilingual poems for primary grades. See other seasonal collections by the same author.

Benke, Karen. *Rip the Page! Adventures in Creative Writing.* Boston: Roost Books, 2010. Poetry writing tips and more. For grades three through twelve.

———*Leap Write In! Adventures in Creative Writing to Stretch and Surprise Your One-of-a-Kind Mind.* Boston: Roost Books, 2013. For tweens, teens, and older.

California Poets in the Schools: annual statewide anthologies of youth poetry. Website: www.cpits.org. Kindergarten through grade twelve.

Center for the Art of Translation. *The Best of Poetry Inside Out.* A series of bilingual anthologies, written and translated by student poets. Website: www.catranslation.org.

Edgar, Christopher, and Ron Padgett. *Educating the Imagination*, vols. 1 and 2. New York: Teachers & Writers Collaborative, 1994. About third grade and up.

Fagin, Larry. *The List Poem: A Guide to Teaching and Writing Catalog Verse.* New York: Teachers & Writers Collaborative, 2000. All ages.

Herrera, Juan Felipe. *Laughing Out Loud, I Fly.* New York: Joanna Cotler Books, 1998. Bilingual; for grades three through twelve.

Hughes, Langston. *The Dream Keeper and Other Poems.* New York: Knopf Books for Young Readers, 1996. For kindergarten through grade twelve.

Intrator, Sam M., and Megan Scribner. *Teaching with Fire: Poetry that Sustains the Courage to Teach.* San Francisco, CA: Jossey Bass, 2003. Secondary through adult.

Koch, Kenneth. *Rose, Where Did You Get That Red? Teaching Great Poetry to Children.* New York: Vintage Books, 1974. For kindergarten through grade six.

———*Wishes, Lies and Dreams: Teaching Children to Write Poetry.* New York: Harper and Row, 1970. For kindergarten through grade twelve.

Kowit, Steve. *In the Palm of Your Hand: The Poet's Portable Workshop.* Gardiner, ME: Tilbury House Publishers, 1995. Secondary through adult.

Krieger, David. *Never Enough Flowers: The Poetry of Peace II.* Santa Barbara, CA: CreateSpace Independent Publishing Platform, 2012. Adult and youth poems.

Lomax, Dana Teen. *Kindergarde: Avant-Garde Stories, Plays, Poems, and Songs for Children.* Lafayette, CA: Black Radish Books, 2013. Children of all ages.

Michael, Pamela, ed., and Robert Hass. *Young Poets and Artists on the Nature of Things.* Minneapolis: Milkweed Editions, 2008.

———*River of Words Environmental Poetry and Art for Youth.* Educators' Guide.: River of Words, 2001. Kindergarden through grade twelve.

Myers, Tim J. *Basho and the Fox.* Amazon Children's Publishing, 2000. For age five and up.

Nye, Naomi Shihab. *The Space Between Our Footsteps: Poems and Paintings from the Middle East.* New York: Simon & Schuster Children's Publishing, 1998. For grades four and up.

Padgett, Ron, ed. *Handbook of Poetic Forms.* New York: Teachers & Writers Collaborative, 2000. As essential as a dictionary! For all ages.

Sweeney, Jacqueline. *Teaching Poetry: Yes You Can!* New York: Scholastic, 1999. For grades four through eight.

Teachers & Writers Collaborative. Magazine and Website: www.twc.org.

Wooldridge, Susan. *poemcrazy: freeing your life with words.* New York: Random House, 1996. For secondary through adult.

Yep, Laurence. *American Dragons: Twenty-five Asian Voices.* New York: Harper Collins, 1995. For grades eight through twelve.

Young, Sue. *The New Comprehensive American Rhyming Dictionary.* New York: Collins Reference, 1991. For grades five and up.

Our Mission

Founded in 1964, California Poets in the Schools is one of the largest literary artists-in-residence programs in the nation. We encourage students throughout California to recognize and celebrate their creativity, intuition, and intellectual curiosity through the creative poetry writing process. We provide students with a multicultural community of published poets, specially trained to bring their experience and love for their craft into the classroom. CPitS serves 25,000 students annually in hundreds of public and private schools, juvenile halls, after-school programs, hospitals, and other community settings. We also partner with the California Arts Council to share the Poetry Out Loud recitation program with high schools and audiences throughout the state.

To support us or find other resources for young writers, please contact us:

California Poets in the Schools
1333 Balboa Street, Suite 3
San Francisco, California 94118
Office: 415-221-4201
info@cpits.org
www.cpits.org

Coming Soon to a High School Near You!

Poetry Out Loud, presented in partnership with the California Arts Council, the National Endowment for the Arts, and the Poetry Foundation, is a national program that encourages high school students to learn about great poetry through memorization, performance, and competition.

Poetry Out Loud is a natural complement to creative writing workshops.

To sign up your school please contact California Poets in the Schools or the California Arts Council. We are partnering to bring this extraordinary opportunity to all California high schools statewide.

info@cpits.org (Tina Pasquinzo)
kmargolis@cac.ca.gov (Kristin Margolis)
www.cac.ca.gov/poetryoutloud